THIS CURSED WAR

Daniel McDonald Jr.

May 30, 2019

Acknowledgements

My mother Lorena McDonald Johnson instilled in our family a reverence for our ancestors who, like Lachlan McIntosh, immigrated from the Highlands of Scotland to the low country of colonial Georgia. One of our ancestors, again like Lachlan McIntosh, served in the Continental army during the American Revolution, participating in the sieges of Savannah and Charleston.

I spent many weeks visiting my grandparents Daniel E. and Lorena "Nina" Beckett McDonald in McIntosh County, Georgia. They imparted an appreciation for the landscape where Lachlan McIntosh lived. Their neighbor Bessie Lewis fired my imagination with local lore and, even though she passed away many years ago, continues to inform me through her books and newspaper columns.

McIntosh descendent Mattie Gladstone of the Ridge near Darien shared her notes and showed me historic sites. Billy McIntosh of Savannah guided me around town and pinpointed the site of Lachlan McIntosh's duel.

I am indebted to many librarians for helping me obtain books, articles and various ancient, obscure or rare materials. I particularly want to thank Amber Gibbs Cook and her colleagues in the interlibrary loan department at the University of South Carolina.

THIS CURSED WAR

Lachlan McIntosh
in the American Revolution

DANIEL McDONALD JOHNSON

Daniel McDonald Johnson
Allendale, South Carolina

2018

ISBN   978-0-692-99618-8

Daniel McDonald Johnson
Post Office Box 747
Allendale, South Carolina 29810

www.danielmcdonaldjohnson.com

'This cursed war has ruined us all.'

Robert Baillie to Lachlan McIntosh, July 17, 1781.

Papers of Lachlan McIntosh (Savannah: Georgia Historical Society, 1957), 99.

About the Author

Daniel McDonald Johnson spent twenty-five years writing for newspapers and now works as a librarian at the University of South Carolina Salkehatchie. He has written several books concerning Clan Mackintosh and McIntosh families.

BLOOD ON THE MARSH is a sprawling epic that traces McIntosh and McDonald families from their ancestral home in the Scottish Highlands to the southern frontier of Colonial America, and describes their participation in the Jacobite Risings and the American Revolution.

MR. MCINTOSH'S FAMILY deals with Clan Mackintosh in the Jacobite Risings and with the McIntosh families who settled Darien, Georgia, and fought in the struggle for the Colonial American southern frontier.

BRIER CREEK BATTLEGROUND gives the history and legend of a Revolutionary War site near Sylvania, Georgia. The book includes maps, photos and travel information for people who want to visit the battleground and related sites along the Savannah River. Biographical information is given on John McIntosh, who was taken prisoner at Brier Creek.

Table of Contents

Author's Note

In writing this work of narrative nonfiction, I have used quotations from letters, journals and other primary sources as a substitute for the dialogue that would appear in a work of fiction. To keep the narrative flowing without typographical distractions, I have converted eighteenth-century conventions of capitalization, punctuation and spelling to present-day standards. Readers who wish to see the unvarnished primary sources may refer to the notes and bibliography at the end of this book.

THIS CURSED WAR

1

Exposed by Land and Water to Enemies

Threats arose from three directions. British East Florida provided a stronghold for enemy forces near Georgia's southern border; Indians influenced by British agents roamed the western frontier; warships patrolled the coast. Lachlan McIntosh assessed the threats and concentrated on preparing Savannah to repulse an attack.

McIntosh learned seven ships lurked outside the Savannah harbor, with six hundred sailors, soldiers and marines ready to raid upriver. He reported to George Washington that the British "meant to land at or near the town, destroy it, and carry off about twenty sail of shipping lying in the river, having, among other articles, near three thousand tierces of rice on board."[1] He sent detachments to defensive positions at Causton's Bluff, Half Moon Bluff and Thunderbolt. He assigned guards to landing sites along the river. He prepared ambushes along the roads leading into town.

In February of 1776 the war of the American Revolution had just begun; the battles of Lexington and Concord had launched the war ten months earlier; Georgia patriots had expelled Britain's government within the past few months and the royal governor had recently escaped to a British ship; the Continental Congress would not declare independence for another five months. Congress had approved a Continental battalion in Georgia and McIntosh had been appointed to command it, but only thirty men had been recruited. Savannah, McIntosh told Washington, was "open, straggling, defenseless and deserted." In response to "this desperate state of affairs," McIntosh "ventured to take command of the militia, lest the colony should be tamely given up, though, I must acknowledge, with some reluctance."[2] McIntosh would defend Savannah with fewer than three hundred Georgia militiamen and about one hundred South Carolina militiamen.

As McIntosh expected, the British fleet sailed upriver to within two and a half miles of Savannah. When the fleet halted in front of Brewton Plantation, McIntosh placed a detachment of 150 men commanded by Colonel Archibald Bulloch on the plantation. The British "were parading with their boats for several days" but did not attempt to land troops.[3]

On the evening of March 2, a British transport ship, a sloop and several armed boats sailed behind Hutchinson's Island, which divides the Savannah River in front of the town of Savannah. The maneuver kept the vessels out of range of an artillery battery overlooking the river; the artillery fired on the vessels but did no damage. McIntosh thought the British vessels would come around Hutchinson's Island and land troops at the village of Yamacraw, a short distance upriver of Savannah. He ordered a battery of three four-pound artillery pieces "erected in haste" at Yamacraw, "threw up entrenchments," and sent soldiers to guard the landing. To prevent the British from stealing the merchant ships loaded with rice that were anchored on the Savannah side of Hutchinson's Island, the Georgia government "resolved the shipping should not sail, and ordered they should be unrigged."[4] The order, however, was not carried out immediately.

The British deceived McIntosh by landing three hundred British soldiers on the far side of Hutchinson's Island where they could not be seen from Savannah. Despite the darkness of night and the cold of early spring, they maneuvered through muddy marsh studded with sawgrass, swampy land tangled with undergrowth, and shallow water of meandering creeks. McIntosh believed the British received assistance from "our own seafaring people, and many from the town."[5] When the British soldiers reached the near side of the island, they hid aboard merchant ships that were anchored beside the island. The dead-of-night maneuver prevented the Georgians from knowing that the British had taken possession of the merchant ships.

Joseph Rice rowed out from Savannah to disable the merchant ships at Hutchinson's Island as ordered by the Georgia government. Rice intended to strip the sails and remove the rudders from the merchant ships, which were called riceboats because they were loaded with a cargo of rice. The British soldiers who had boarded the riceboats during the night surprised Rice and took him prisoner. McIntosh still did not know that the British troops were on Hutchinson's Island.

Early on Sunday morning, March 3, a British schooner and a sloop, armed with eight or ten guns each, sailed around the end of Hutchinson's Island and came down the river between the island and the town. McIntosh believed the armed vessels had come to cover a troop landing on the mainland. Parties of militia commanded by Major Joseph Habersham trained small arms fire on the warships. The battle "kept smartly engaged on both sides most of the day."[6]

Two American sailors risked their lives by sneaking away from Hutchinson's Island, coming ashore in Savannah and informing McIntosh that the British were holding prisoner the man who had been sent to disable the riceboats. McIntosh sent Raymond Demere II and Daniel Roberts "to go only alongside the vessels, and, without arms, to demand our fellow-citizen, Mr. Rice; but, to our astonishment, they were also forced on board and kept."[7]

Later in the morning, a dozen Georgia riflemen led by Captain John Baker rowed into the river and opened fire on the British. When McIntosh ordered the patriot battery at Yamacraw to open fire, the British ships returned fire. The battle raged throughout the afternoon.

When the patriots in Savannah learned that the captains of several merchant ships were cooperating with the British, they "were inflamed, particularly at our own people who had treacherously joined the enemy against us." The patriots considered sending a party to board the ships "but we had neither boats, sailors or arms proper for the attempt," McIntosh reported. "The general cry then was to set all the shipping on fire."[8]

McIntosh faced a hard choice. As the military commander, he realized the only way to prevent the British from obtaining provisions was to destroy the riceboats. As a planter who grew rice on the South Georgia coast, he knew the rice crop generated significant wealth for Georgia's landowners and merchants. He chose to burn the riceboats. At his direction, men applied a coat of pitch to the mast, spars, and rigging of a confiscated ship valued at £20,000. They set the pitch ablaze, and sent the fire ship drifting toward the riceboats. The fire ship ran aground and became a beacon in the evening sky. McIntosh persevered, preparing a sloop as a fire ship and propelling it toward the riceboats. This fire ship rammed two riceboats, setting them afire.

The crews of ten riceboats cut free from their anchors as the patriots fired on them with artillery and rifles. The British armed vessels escorted the riceboats upriver on an incoming tide. British soldiers on Hutchinson's Island scrambled to dodge shots fired by patriots on the shore at Savannah, "running in the marsh in a laughable manner for fear of our rifles though far past their reach."[9] The British soldiers found refuge on boats out of range of the American artillery. The British fleet and the ten merchant ships loaded with sixteen hundred barrels of rice moved behind the cover of Hutchinson's Island and retreated downriver to Tybee Island.

McIntosh reported that three patriots had been wounded in the series of engagements that became known as the Battle of the Riceboats. He thought the British "must have many both killed and wounded, though they acknowledge but six. Several were seen to fall."[10]

Throughout the night after the Battle of the Riceboats ended, the fire ship and the two riceboats it had set afire drifted up and down the river with the tide. Flames darted into the night sky and reflected in the glossy surface of the Savannah River as the burning vessels passed Savannah in one direction and later, after the tide changed, floated past the town in the opposite direction.

When morning came, Lachlan arranged for the riceboats that remained in Savannah after the battle to be moved to a location where they could be closely guarded. The British and the patriots agreed to a cessation of hostilities. The patriots confined several British sympathizers until the British released Demere, Roberts and Rice.

"Whether they intend to try us again or not, I am not able to inform Your Excellency," McIntosh told Washington. "In this I think they rather lost more than gained any reputation, and have done us great honor by being the second province on the continent which they have attacked and were shamefully foiled."[11]

The British fleet abandoned Georgia a few days later, leaving only two ships to observe the Savannah harbor.[12]

After the crisis of the Battle of the Riceboats, McIntosh concentrated on recruiting for Georgia's Continental battalion. Many Georgians would not leave their farms and families to join the army. Low pay and a lower enlistment bounty than offered in nearby South Carolina hampered recruitment efforts. McIntosh recruited a little more than three hundred men for Georgia's Continental battalion, only half as many as authorized by Congress. About six hundred militiamen assisted the Continental battalion in defending Georgia. Realizing that Georgia could not defend itself, Congress formed a Southern Military Department headquartered in Charleston and tasked with defending Georgia and the other southern states.

Unlike any other southern state, Georgia bordered on British-held territory. British troops, loyalists and Indians operating out of British East Florida raided the sparsely populated plantations and villages of South Georgia almost with impunity. McIntosh sent a troop of sixty horsemen commanded by his older brother William McIntosh to patrol the southern border. Another troop of sixty horsemen patrolled the western frontier, where Indians allied with the British threatened backcountry settlements.

British officials in Florida responded by sending a military unit to guard the crossings on the St. Mary's River, arming the loyalist settlers on the border, and stationing a schooner in the St. Mary's. The British moved cattle from southern Georgia and northern Florida to the area south of the St. John's, out of the patriot raiders' reach.

The British authorized a troop of rangers to operate along the border. Thomas Brown, a loyalist who had fled Georgia after being tortured by patriots in Augusta, recruited the rangers from the backcountry of Georgia and South Carolina. The British also sought assistance from Indian trading partners.

In May of 1776 William McIntosh led a raid into British East Florida. Although the raiders confronted a strong British fort on the St. Mary's River, they succeeded in capturing nearly twenty prisoners, burning plantations,

destroying provisions, and carrying off slaves and cattle.
British pursuers caught up with the raiders as they returned
across the St. Mary's to Georgia. The opponents exchanged
fire across the river, wounding three Georgians and killing
one British soldier. Three of the loyalist plantation owners
escaped during the fight. Later that night, a British party
crossed the river in a small boat and rescued three more
loyalist planters.[13]

To defend Georgia against British forces in Florida,
William McIntosh began building forts on the Altamaha
and the St. Mary's. Continental officer Samuel Elbert
reported that Lachlan McIntosh had gone to "our southern
frontiers on some important business" in May,[14] indicating
that Lachlan may have joined William while the forts were
built. A detachment from the Georgia battalion guarded
crossings on the Altamaha. Georgia established a
stronghold at the southern port of Sunbury with a fort,
ditches, earthworks, artillery, twenty men from the Georgia
Continental battalion and forty residents designated as
minute men.

Lachlan McIntosh's friend and business partner Henry
Laurens of Charleston checked on his investments in
coastal Georgia as warfare swept through the area. Laurens
spent the month of May at his New Hope plantation and at
his plantation on Broughton Island adjoining property
belonging to the McIntosh brothers.[15]

The Georgia Council of Safety panicked when rumors arose that British troops and Indian allies were advancing from Florida toward the Georgia border. The president of the Council, Archibald Bulloch, ordered all detachments of the Georgia battalion to rush to the defense of Savannah, leaving parish militia to defend the border. Bulloch pleaded with Lachlan McIntosh to stop the invaders at the Satilla River if possible and to fall back to the Altamaha only if absolutely necessary. The rumors of an invasion, however, turned out to be a false alarm.[16]

As raiding continued, thousands of cattle were driven back and forth across the border. In one instance, when four thousand cattle were stolen from a plantation in South Georgia, the caretaker accused Scots settlers of assisting the British.[17]

Continental General Charles Lee arrived in Charleston in the summer of 1776 to take command of the Southern Military Department. Lachlan McIntosh led a delegation from Georgia to meet with Lee to devise a defensive strategy. While the delegates were in Charleston, they witnessed a British assault on the city.

A fleet of fifty British vessels, including troop transports, anchored near Charleston in early June. Over several days, 2,500 British troops went ashore on an island to the north of Sullivan's Island. The British troops launched an attack across a breach separating them from Sullivan's Island but were foiled because the surface of the breach concealed holes too deep to wade through and shoals too shallow to row across. American defenders put up a spirited defense and drove the British back. The British abandoned plans for an amphibious assault and put their faith in a naval assault.

On June 28, William Moultrie wrote, British ships of war began the attack on Fort Sullivan "most furiously" at 10 in the morning and "continued a brisk fire" until 8 at night. Many shells fell into the fort but "we had a morass in the middle that swallowed them up instantly, and those that fell in the sand in and about the fort were immediately buried so that very few of them bursted amongst us." The British bombardment "could not make any impression on our fort, built of palmetto logs and filled in with earth, our merlons were 16 feet thick, and high enough to cover the men from the fire of the tops." The twelve men who were killed and the twenty-four who were wounded "received their shots mostly through the embrasures."[18]

Moultrie said his men "fought bravely" despite harsh conditions. "It being a very hot day, we were served along the platform with grog in fire-buckets, which we partook of very heartily: I never had a more agreeable draught than that which I took out of one of those buckets at the time; it may be very easily conceived what heat and thirst a man must feel in this climate, to be upon a platform on the 28th June, amidst twenty or thirty heavy pieces of cannon, in one continual blaze and roar; and clouds of smoke curling over his head for hours together; it was a very honorable situation, but a very unpleasant one."[19]

Moultrie recorded the legendary deed of Sergeant William Jasper, a Georgian serving in the 2nd South

Carolina Regiment. "During the action, thousands of our fellow-citizens were looking on from Charleston, about six miles away from Fort Sullivan, with anxious hopes and fears, some of whom had their fathers, brothers, and husbands in the battle; whose hearts must have been pierced at every broad-side. After some time our flag was shot away; their hopes were then gone, and they gave up all for lost! supposing that we had struck our flag, and had given up the fort: Sergeant Jasper perceiving that the flag was shot away, and had fallen without the fort, jumped from one of the embrasures, and brought it up through a heavy fire, fixed it upon a sponge-staff, and planted it upon the ramparts again: Our flag once more waving in the air, revived the drooping spirits of our friends; and they continued looking on until night had closed the scene and hid us from their view."[20]

During the night, the British called off the attack and moved their ships out of range of the American artillery. "When the firing had ceased," Moultrie reported, "our friends for a time were again in an unhappy suspense, not knowing our fate; until they received an account by a dispatch boat, which I sent up to town, to acquaint them, that the British ships had retired, and that we were victorious."[21]

McIntosh called the victory at Charleston "glorious" and congratulated "our friends and country on our happy success."[22]

With Charleston safe, General Lee focused on the strategic importance of the southern frontier. Lee knew that Georgia did not have the resources to protect the border with British East Florida. Lee asked Congress to send more troops to Georgia and proposed that a cavalry force be created in Georgia. He also sent the 2nd South Carolina Regiment to Purrysburg on the South Carolina side of the Savannah River just upstream from Savannah. Congress authorized two more battalions, four row galleys, two artillery companies and a regiment of rangers for the defense of Georgia.

Because duties in Savannah and Charleston consumed nearly all of Lachlan McIntosh's time and attention, his eighteen-year-old son Lackie accepted responsibility for protecting the family home and property in the Darien area. As part of his responsibility, Lackie protected his mother, three of his younger brothers and his two sisters; the older sister was about five years old in the summer of 1776. Lackie's nineteen-year-old brother John, called Jack, was staying with his uncle John Mackintosh in Jamaica.[23] Lackie's seventeen-year-old brother William was stationed in Savannah as an ensign in the 5th Regiment, while Lackie commanded a company of the Georgia battalion that was stationed at Darien in mid-July.[24]

Lackie wrote his father on July 22 to report that everyone in the family was "in perfect health" and that the younger McIntosh children were coming on "very fast indeed with their schooling" but needed some spelling books and primers.[25]

Plantation business was "going on very well" despite the constant threat of raids from privateers based in St. Augustine. The plantation had "a very fine crop of rice upon the ground," the corn crop was "pretty good," but the potato crop was "but poor."[26] Lackie was supervising the construction of a 20-foot by 30-foot barn made of squared logs.

Upon being alerted that a notorious privateer had sailed into the Darien area, Lackie pledged "to keep up as strict a guard as if I expected him hourly." The troops posted at Darien were "very satisfied" and "quite content with their rations" and a half pint of rum three times a week. The troops, however, "were sent here without cartridge boxes" and were "obliged to put their cartridges in their pockets, which makes it very inconvenient."[27]

Lackie wrote his father, "I am sorry you can't take a step home at this time, however it was a thing impossible as you expected General Lee, and another Battalion of Continental Troops. I should like much to be there, at the time of their coming in, they will make a fine show."[28]

Lachlan McIntosh informed Lee of turmoil in South Georgia. Indians and Floridians destroyed one plantation and robbed another, and attacked the eighteen patriots defending Fort Barrington on the Altamaha River. The residents of South Georgia "are in the utmost confusion, no militia can be had as they are busy moving their families," McIntosh told Lee. "I must set off immediately to the southward with what few horsemen I can collect. I am in haste, Sir."[29]

In late July, William McIntosh's force encountered British soldiers from St. Augustine and their Indian allies on the St. Mary's River. The botanist William Bartram, a longtime friend of the McIntosh family, may have acted as a volunteer scout for William McIntosh at the time but would not enlist because of his Quaker beliefs.[30]

"Hostilities commenced by the parties firing at each other across the river," Bartram wrote. "The British were under cover of the evacuated trading houses, and the Georgians shielded themselves behind the trees, on the river banks. The conflict had continued for some time when the Chief of the Indians threw down his gun and boldly stepping out from the corner of a house he took off his hat and whirling it up in the air as he advanced to the river side, amidst showers of bullets, he spoke aloud to the Georgians, declaring that they were brothers and friends and that he knew not any cause why they should spill each other's blood. Neither I (said he) nor my companions the Red Men, will fire another gun. He turned about, shouted, and immediately led off the Indians."[31]

Patriot forces patrolling the frontier, Lachlan McIntosh reported, "had no artillery, many of their horses were stolen, and most of the officers as well as the men were jaded and tired out – and bad weather. In the meantime, about two thousand head of cattle were carried off by two troops of horse the enemy have lately raised in East Florida. I heartily wish the settlements of the country [British East Florida] were entirely broken up and confined to their castle [the formidable fort in St. Augustine]. It would give the colony [Georgia] some rest from their pilferers by land and water, and detach the Creek Indians from their interest."[32]

McIntosh's hearty wish came true. On July 30, the Georgia Council of Safety recommended that he lead an expedition into East Florida. He crossed the Altamaha in early August and raided every settlement north of the St. John's River. His troops laid waste to crops, took cattle, and confiscated slaves. McIntosh delegated a division to attack Wright's Fort, a stronghold on the St. Mary's River. The British garrison was taken by surprise and surrendered. The raids struck terror in Florida settlers, who accused McIntosh of behaving in a "most cruel and wanton manner." As he had hoped, the settlers fled to St. Augustine. When McIntosh led his troops back to the north side of the Altamaha, the Floridians were not sure the incursion was over; they suspected McIntosh would gather fresh supplies and renew the offensive. McIntosh, however, had accomplished his mission. He returned to Savannah.[33]

A copy of the Declaration of Independence arrived in Savannah on August 10. A crowd in the square outside the Georgia Assembly house cheered when the Declaration was read. The grenadier and light infantry companies fired a volley. The provost-martial mounted his horse, drew his sword and led a procession to the liberty pole, where the Declaration was read once again. The Georgia Continental battalion joined the local militia in discharging field pieces and firing in platoons. The burgeoning crowd of civilians and soldiers surged to the Trustees' Gardens, where the

Declaration was read once again and the cannon of the battery roared a salute.

Lachlan McIntosh was among the political leaders, influential citizens and militia officers who dined under a canopy of cedar trees. McIntosh and his colleagues cheerfully drank a toast to the new United States of America.

As evening fell, the town was illuminated. The largest crowd that had ever gathered in Georgia witnessed a mock funeral procession, complete with fifes and muffled drums, signifying the end of British rule.[34]

Southern Department commander Charles Lee arrived in Savannah early in August with about fifteen hundred Continental troops from Virginia, North Carolina and South Carolina. Acting on a recommendation by the Continental Congress, Lee prepared to invade British East Florida with a goal of capturing St. Augustine. Lee returned to Charleston and placed General William Moultrie of the 2nd South Carolina Regiment in charge of the invasion. Georgia failed to support the invasion with equipment, clothing and shoes for the invading force, inspiring Lee's caustic comment that the Georgians would propose "mounting a body of Mermaids on Alligators."[35] Lee, however, respected Lachlan McIntosh and described the 1st Battalion of Foot under McIntosh's command as one of the best battalions in America.[36]

The attempt to take St. Augustine was doomed to fail. When the Continental troops sickened in coastal Georgia's semi-tropical climate, the Georgians did not provide medical supplies; as a result, the death rate was fourteen or fifteen a day. The main body of American troops had advanced no farther than Sunbury when the invasion collapsed in mid-September. The departing troops left Sunbury in shambles.[37]

In the midst of the invasion, Congress gave Lee a new assignment. Brigadier James Moore of North Carolina was named commander of the Southern Department. General Robert Howe was given command of Continental forces in South Carolina and Georgia. When Lee left Georgia, he took some of the South Carolina units with him.

While Lachlan McIntosh maintained headquarters in Savannah, his wife and children remained on the perilous southern frontier. Unremitting military emergencies prevented Lachlan from checking on his family in Darien. "I am sorry to find you are disappointed in coming home, as we have been expecting you for this week past," his teenage son Lackie wrote. "However we shall look for you daily."

Lackie sent his father news about the family. Lachlan's five-year-old daughter Esther, called Hetty, had suffered from a fever for several days but was getting better. Hetty and Lachlan's wife Sarah were "very fond" of necklaces Lachlan had sent them, Lackie said, because the necklaces were "American produce."

The family livelihood depended on its planting operation even in the midst of a war zone, and Lackie kept

Lachlan posted on developments. "We have as fine a crop of rice as you would ever desire to see," Lackie boasted. "We shall have some fit to cut in less than three weeks."[1]

In addition to reporting on family affairs as a son to his father, Lackie also reported on military affairs as a captain to his commanding officer. "As it is inconvenient for you to send a command to relieve me, I am very well satisfied as I find all the command excepting three or four are quite contented to stay another month. The only thing I have to complain of is that a detachment of men should be sent to so dangerous a post as this without a plenty of ammunition. I have but a small keg of cartridges Lieut. Handley brought here, not more than five or six rounds at most apiece for the men and not one single man has a cartridge box. We had an alarm a few days ago. They were obliged to carry their ammunition in their pockets, which was very unhandy in case they had been engaged. However, I shall endeavor to make out another month with what ammunition I have. I believe we shan't be in want as I may get some powder from Captain Thredcraft belonging to the militia in case of necessity."[1]

Lackie informed Lachlan that slaves had been carried away from a Darien plantation belonging to Henry Laurens and that five or six of William McIntosh's best horses had been stolen.[1]

"I wish you could send my horse home as he is much wanted," Lackie added.[1]

Ten days later, Lackie reported that the situation at Darien continued to worsen. "The unhealthy situation of my command just now, obliges me to send an express to acquaint you. I have now six or seven extremely ill with a very violent kind of fever; they have no intermission at all scarcely and last night one of them, a little Scotch boy, died. I can assure you, Sir, it was not the want of care occasioned his death; I spare no pains or expense attending the poor fellows when they are sick, and I keep Doctor Blunt continually with them. I excuse him from all duty on that account."[1]

The troops at Darien "seem to cry out now for to be relieved. I think a change of air will be of service to them. However, I am in hopes no more of them will die, as I give them today plenty of dogwood bark, they seem to be more lively than they were yesterday. If you can't relieve them, they say if they could get some clothes they would be satisfied. Some of them, and indeed almost the whole, I can assure you, have not wherewith to hide their nakedness."[1]

Because his wife and younger children faced constant danger at Darien, Lachlan McIntosh purchased a large house on St. James Square in Savannah for his family. He also transferred slaves from Darien to Savannah.[1]

Lachlan McIntosh's plantation was destroyed not by British raiders but by American troops foraging for food. Lachlan asked Congress to compensate him for the rice, corn, peas and potatoes "taken and destroyed by our own troops who burnt my fences and turned their horses into the fields."[1] As British and American raiders crossed back and forth along the southern frontier, they destroyed Lachlan McIntosh's house, barn and outbuildings.[1]

The McIntosh property had been "more in danger, and exposed by land and water to enemies of every colour and kind," Lachlan McIntosh observed, "than any other citizen perhaps in the United States." His losses included not only all his crops but also all his hogs and about four hundred head of cattle.[1] Twenty-four slaves escaped from his plantation.[1]

Congress continued to take steps to defend the southern frontier by authorizing more Continental forces in Georgia. With the additional manpower, the Georgia battalion commanded by Colonel Lachlan McIntosh would become the Georgia brigade commanded by a brigadier general. Button Gwinnett, one of Georgia's delegates to the Continental Congress, had returned to Georgia after signing the Declaration of Independence and had expected to be appointed to command the new Georgia brigade.

Former friends McIntosh and Gwinnett became rivals, a development that would haunt McIntosh for the rest of his military career. Congress voted to retain McIntosh as commander of Georgia's Continental troops; he received a promotion to brigadier general on September 16, 1776.

The authorization of additional manpower in Georgia was more theoretical than actual. The 538 men in the 1st Battalion of Foot were dispersed in small groups on guard duty around the state. Recruiters strove to fill the ranks of the 2nd and 3rd Battalions. About three hundred horsemen patrolled the frontier and garrisoned Fort Barrington on the Altamaha. The troops lacked barracks, clothes, blankets, medicine, entrenching tools and axes.[38]

British forces from Florida continued to threaten Georgia. McIntosh ordered a troop of horsemen commanded by his older brother William to cross the Altamaha and confront the British.

Acting on reports in early October that the British were planning to invade Georgia by land and sea, Lachlan arrayed his troops in defensive positions along the coast. The South Carolina navy and a detachment of the 2nd South Carolina Regiment helped protect coastal Georgia.

William, who had been promoted to lieutenant colonel, continued to patrol the border with a light horse regiment of about three hundred men. In late October, his troops attacked a British party on the Satilla River, killing one member of the party and capturing two.

Lachlan ordered the Georgians to fall back to Georgia's strongest natural barrier, the Altamaha River. He informed General Robert Howe, the commander of the Continental troops in Georgia and South Carolina, of a plan "to surround our settlements with a chain of stockade forts from the upper settlement on Savannah River to Barrington on the Altamaha."[39]

Lachlan advised William, "As your Regiment of Light Horse is chiefly intended for protecting our back settlements from the incursions of Indians or others, it is my opinion your principal garrison and headquarters should be at Barrington."[40] Small parties went out from Barrington to keep open communication with Darien and to observe enemy activity south of the Altamaha.

On October 27, a party of loyalists and Indian allies destroyed a plantation south of the Altamaha, crossed the river, and attacked Fort Barrington. The eighteen men garrisoning Fort Barrington held off the attackers until William McIntosh's horsemen forced the loyalists and Indians to withdraw.[41]

Other attacks were reported at Midway, Beard's Bluff, and St. Simon's Island. The raiders destroyed the houses and provisions on a plantation south of the Altamaha and burned several small settlements on the north side of the Altamaha near Beard's Bluff, forty miles upriver from Barrington. A hunting party of about twenty Chiaha attacked forty Georgia Rangers, slaying four rangers and wounding two.[42]

Lachlan McIntosh led a relief column from Savannah. As he approached the settlements that had been raided he witnessed "people in the utmost confusion, families, women, children and luggage all along the road as I came." He tried to calm their fears and managed to convince many of them to return to their homes. He sent soldiers to secure the important river crossing at Beard's Bluff, and sent scouting parties south of the Altamaha. He ordered a party to proceed directly to the Satilla River "or even over St. John's River if necessary so that I think they can hardly miss overtaking and chastising the fugitives."[43] He reported, "The South Carolina Horse came a few days too late to overtake the Indians who occasioned the alarm."

McIntosh then gave the South Carolinians a new assignment. "After scouring both sides of the River Altamaha 30 or 40 miles above Barrington, I ordered them to range as far as St. Mary's to protect any persons who

choose to hunt up their cattle."[44]   McIntosh stayed at Fort
Barrington for fourteen days before returning to Savannah.

In December, Indians killed a trooper of the Light
Horse on the frontier. McIntosh ordered Colonel William
McIntosh and Major Leonard Marbury to "hunt the
assassins forever until they come up with them. The Indians
themselves have begun first plundering and now
murdering; therefore I see no cause of sparing them any
longer wherever they are to be found."[45]   Shortly
afterwards, Lachlan McIntosh himself led reinforcements
to Barrington, which had been renamed Fort Howe in honor
of General Robert Howe, and took command. The
operation concluded with the capture of three Indians who
were accused of killing the trooper; they were imprisoned
in Savannah while the accusation was investigated.[46]

The McIntosh brothers worked to improve defensive
positions along the frontier, although the Georgia
convention did not provide funding for adequate
fortifications. Lachlan McIntosh ordered an infantry
attachment to establish positions on the Sapelo River and at
several locations along the Altamaha in the vicinity of
Darien. Still, British raiding parties continued to steal
slaves and plunder property.

When raiders from Florida drove off a herd of cattle, a
party of the Georgia Light Horse pursued them but could
not catch them; while on the Florida side of the St. Mary's
River, the Georgians did some plundering of their own.[47]

As night fell on December 27, Indians wounded a man
outside the Georgia fort at Beard's Bluff. At daybreak,
Lieutenant Jeremiah Bugg led twelve men out of the fort to

find the attackers. The Indians killed four of the men and shot Bugg's horse out from under him.

The surviving men raced back to the fort. Bugg was left behind, but managed to reach safety on foot. The Indians scalped the four dead men and left arrows sticking in them. All of the men stationed at Beard's Bluff deserted except for one who accompanied Bugg to Fort Howe.[48]

On New Year's Day of 1777, a troop of Continental horsemen led by William McIntosh arrived at a strategic location on the Satilla River where they intended to build a stockade to protect Georgia against raids from British East Florida. The troop had been on a defensive expedition through the semi-tropical wilderness for nearly two weeks. While most of the men constructed the fort, twenty-two men guarded the workmen, thirteen men and an officer continuously scouted the area, and eight men guarded the troop's horses. Fifteen men stood watch at night. Because the troop did not have a commissary, a sergeant and six men occasionally brought in cattle and other provisions. A messenger arrived on January 3 to tell William about the attack on the Americans at Beard's Bluff. William departed from the stockade on the Satilla River the next day.[49]

Lachlan McIntosh assigned forty men to reoccupy the fort at Beard's Bluff and sent reinforcements to Fort Howe. Georgia did not provide enough money to pay the soldiers and provide supplies, prompting some of the men to steal civilian property and some of their officers to resign.

Early in the morning of February 17, Florida Rangers and their Indian allies attacked Fort McIntosh on the Satilla River. In seven hours of fighting, one American was killed and three were wounded. Lachlan McIntosh sent out a relief force that halted when Florida Rangers fired upon it. British General L.V. Fuser came up from St. Augustine with 150 regular troops and 120 horsemen to join the siege. The seventy men garrisoning Fort McIntosh surrendered on February 18 when they ran out of ammunition and provisions. The British burned Fort McIntosh and sent parties toward Fort Howe on the Altamaha.

McIntosh responded by stationing a galley in the Altamaha and sending reinforcements to Fort Howe and to Beard's Bluff. He ordered his nephew John McIntosh to leave a small guard at Darien and lead the rest of his command "without delay to Fort Howe (Barrington) and oppose the enemy's progress."[50] Lachlan McIntosh asked Colonel James Screven of Midway to raise as many volunteers as possible and "for God's sake be expeditious."[51] McIntosh ordered Captain John Habersham "to march with all expedition with what men you have to the assistance of Captain Bostick at Fort Howe and prevent, if possible, the enemy's crossing of the Altamaha and entering our settlements."[52] McIntosh himself led troops from Savannah to the Altamaha.[53]

When the British parties reached the Altamaha, McIntosh reported to George Washington, "I met them with the remains of the 1st Battalion (as none of the 2nd had then arrived) and prevented their crossing that river, and entering or doing any mischief in our settlements, with the loss of twelve men."[54]

During the battle, a musket ball struck McIntosh in the heel, inflicting a wound that lingered for two months.

The British regulars retreated to St. Augustine. The Rangers and Indians drove two thousand head of cattle into Florida.[55]

A detachment of the 2nd South Carolina Regiment led by Colonel Isaac Motte and Lieutenant Colonel Francis Marion arrived in Georgia with artillery, naval vessels and provisions. The 2nd South Carolina Regiment returned to Charleston in mid-March, but two hundred troopers in the 3rd Regiment of South Carolina Horse commanded by Colonel Thomas Sumter remained in Georgia.[56]

During the emergency on the border, Georgia's Council of Safety gave all executive power to its president, Archibald Bulloch. When Bulloch suddenly died, Button Gwinnett was elected to be the new president. As president, Gwinnett gained control of the state militia.[57]

From the beginning of the war, Gwinnett had wanted military command and had envied Lachlan McIntosh's position as commander of Georgia's Continental forces. Gwinnett chose to discredit Lachlan McIntosh by smearing the honor of Lachlan's brothers William and George.

It was a fatal decision.

2
Mr. McIntosh's Family

When Lachlan McIntosh was eleven years old, an alligator killed his three-year-old brother Lewis. "At Darien, a most unhappy accident befell Mr. McIntosh's family," an official in Savannah reported, "whose two sons (young lads) being swimming in the river, an alligator snapped one, and carried him quite off."[1] If Lachlan experienced the gruesome sight of Lewis being dragged away in an alligator's jaws, the older brother certainly would have felt both horror and guilt over not being able to protect his little brother.

The young McIntosh lads may not have known the danger lurking in the rivers of coastal Georgia because they had recently arrived on the Colonial American southern frontier. They were natives of the Highlands of Scotland. Their father John Mackintosh, distinguished by the Gaelic word "mor" because of his large size, was part of a leading family in the Borlum branch of Clan Mackintosh. His wife Marjory was a daughter of John Fraser of Garthmore. Their first child, William, was born at Borlum. Lachlan, their second child, was born March 5, 1727, at Achugcha.

In 1735 John Mackintosh Mor led a contingent of Clan Mackintosh and other Highlanders to the newly-formed colony of Georgia. Colonial leader James Oglethorpe directed the Highlanders to settle on the Altamaha River, a strategic location during conflicts between Spanish colonists of Florida and English colonists of South Carolina. The Highlanders named their town Darien.

Lachlan's youngest brother was born May 24, 1739, and was named George in recognition of his birthplace in Georgia. Marjory and John Mackintosh Mor now had seven surviving children: William, age thirteen; Lachlan, twelve; John, eleven; Phineas, seven; Mary Ann, called Ann, two; and infant George.[2] Lachlan was "of athletic form and great activity," an early Georgia historian wrote, and "there was not an Indian in all the tribes that could compete with him in the race"[3]

Warfare on the Colonial American southern frontier disrupted the family. General Oglethorpe received a letter from King George predicting war between England and Spain and instructing Oglethorpe to "annoy" the Spanish forces in Florida. At his military headquarters at Frederica on St. Simon's Island, Oglethorpe recruited a troop of Highland Rangers among immigrants along the Georgia coast, and authorized John Mackintosh Mor to form the Highland Independent Company of Foot at Darien. The seventy men serving under Mackintosh wore plaids or kilts and wielded traditional Highland weapons.

As Mackintosh prepared to go to war in February of 1740, he and his wife placed their son Lachlan and their daughter Ann in the orphanage at Bethesda near Savannah. Lachlan was on the verge of turning thirteen and Ann was no older than three. John and Marjory may have sent Ann to safety because she was the only girl in the family. Since family tradition holds that Marjory wanted her sons to be well educated, she may have viewed Bethesda as a boarding school for Lachlan.[4] The children studied reading and writing for four hours every day, and spent countless hours praying, singing hymns and listening to sermons. They also did chores and learned trades. They followed a strict schedule from arising at five in the morning until going to bed at nine at night. An official at the orphanage reported "no time is allowed for idleness or play, which are Satan's darling hours to tempt children to all manner of wickedness, as lying, cursing, swearing, uncleanness &c., so that though we are about seventy in family yet we hear no more noise than if it was a private house."[5]

When the British invasion of Florida got underway, John Mackintosh Mor's fourteen-year-old son William sneaked out of Darien, traveled with some of his Indian friends, and joined the Highland Independent Company of Foot on the march; his father could not send him back home because they were too far inside enemy territory.[6]

John Mackintosh Mor was taken prisoner in the Battle of Fort Mosa near St. Augustine on June 15, 1740. He did not know the fate of his son William, who managed to jump from the wall of the fort and escape into the semi-tropical wilderness.[7]

After Oglethorpe withdrew from Florida, young William McIntosh remained with the British regiment at Frederica. Marjory Mackintosh took her youngest three sons to Palachacola, a British fort on the Savannah River commanded by her husband's distant kinsman John

Mackintosh. Lachlan McIntosh and his sister Ann remained in the orphanage at Bethesda.

"The Spirit of the Lord I hope is beginning to blow among the dry bones here," Lachlan wrote while staying at Bethesda. "The house was never since I came thither likelier to answer to the end of its institution than now: Little boys and little girls, at this and that corner, crying unto the Lord, that he would have mercy upon them."[8]

After about two years at Palachacola, Marjory Mackintosh retrieved her daughter Ann from the orphanage and carried her younger children back to Darien. Lachlan left the orphanage and joined the regiment at Frederica, reuniting with his brother William.

While Lachlan and William were stationed at Frederica, their regiment fought against Spanish forces that invaded St. Simon's Island. William, age sixteen, fought in the Battle of Bloody Marsh on July 7, 1742, but Lachlan, age fifteen, was assigned to stand guard and herd cattle.[9] That was the extent of Lachlan McIntosh's military service prior to the American Revolution. He learned the rudiments of military organization, however, and he was fortunate to have General Oglethorpe as a mentor and role model. An essay written in the nineteenth century by William's grandson Thomas Spalding claimed the McIntosh brothers "were well instructed in English under their mother's care, and after they were received under the patronage of General Oglethorpe, were instructed in mathematics, and other branches necessary for their future military course."[10]

John Mackintosh Mor was released in a prisoner exchange and returned to Darien late in 1743. He retained his military rank, continued his occupation as a gentleman farmer and also operated a store. Lachlan lived in the family home at Darien and probably helped with the farming and storekeeping until he reached the age of twenty-one.[11]

In 1748 Lachlan and his eleven-year-old brother George went to Charleston, South Carolina. Lachlan made a good impression in his new surroundings, according to biographer Harvey Jackson:

> Nearly six feet tall, athletic, described by one friend as the "handsomest man he had ever seen," and possessing a ready wit that in later, more reserved, years would be seen only by close associates, young Lachlan McIntosh began to make friends and slowly wind his way through the labyrinth of Charleston society. His efforts found an influential ally when, during his third year in the city, he met Henry Laurens. A rising member of the merchant elite and a man of considerable political promise, Laurens took a genuine liking to the Georgian, invited him into his home, and, though only three years McIntosh's senior, became a guiding force in his career. It was a relationship which grew into a long business association, produced a political alliance, and, most importantly, gave Lachlan McIntosh one of the most loyal friendships he was to experience outside his family.[12]

With young men like Lachlan working as clerks in the counting house, Henry Laurens' commercial complex adjoining a wharf on the Cooper River amounted to an early American business school.[13] "Mr. Laurens took the young McIntosh into his counting-house and into his family, and with him he remained some years," Lachlan's grandnephew Thomas Spalding later wrote. "In association with this enlightened and respectable gentleman, Mr. McIntosh had an opportunity of studying men and books, and of filling up the blanks in his education."[14] Lachlan and George were living in the Laurens household when Henry Laurens' son John was born in 1754.

Lachlan's employment not only paid his own bills but also supported his much-younger brother George. When they first arrived in Charleston, Lachlan paid for George to attend grammar school. Lachlan then arranged for George to serve as an apprentice to an architect for four years, and provided "pocket money" amounting to a hundred pounds of South Carolina currency a year. Lachlan purchased an enslaved young black man to "attend on" George, Lachlan later wrote, and "to be brought up in the same business as himself."[15]

A disaster called "the great hurricane" struck Charleston in the autumn of 1752. Strong winds blew in from the northeast on September 14, and by the next morning a howling storm engulfed Charleston. The eye of the hurricane crossed Charleston Harbor as the tide was coming in, causing the water to surge ten feet taller than a typical high tide. The raging wind and water annihilated all the wharves along the harbor and washed ships into the streets. Many buildings collapsed and the rest suffered severe damage. Roofs were torn away, windows were blown out, doors were ripped from their hinges, and chimneys were reduced to rubble. Along a forty-mile swath extending from Charleston, the storm destroyed crops, swept away roads and bridges, knocked down barns, and flattened forests. The storm killed twenty-eight people, according to records, and other deaths went unrecorded.[16]

While Lachlan and George McIntosh were in Charleston, their seventeen-year-old brother Phineas died in Darien. The Frederica regiment was disbanded in 1749 and the company that had been garrisoning the fort at Darien was eliminated; as a result, John Mackintosh Mor was no longer needed as a lieutenant in the company. Shortly after the regiment disbanded, John Mackintosh Mor's third son John Mackintosh, who kept the old spelling of the family name, moved to Jamaica. He established a home, Hermitage, in St. Thomas East and never returned to Georgia, although he corresponded regularly with his family. William was the only son of John Mackintosh Mor remaining in the family homeland on the South-Georgia coast.[17]

Changes to the government of Georgia and related changes to policies on slavery created an opportunity for Lachlan and George to return from South Carolina. The trustees who had governed the settlement of Georgia forbade slavery, a policy the Highlanders who settled

Darien had supported. After the trustees relinquished Georgia to the British crown, large-scale slaveholding was allowed in Georgia. Highlanders who had opposed slavery in the 1730s became slave owners in the 1750s and established extensive plantations in coastal Georgia. Lachlan McIntosh, his brothers George and William, his sister Ann and his father John Mackintosh Mor all received land grants near Darien.

Lachlan moved to Darien shortly after marrying Sarah Threadcraft of Williamsburg, South Carolina, on New Year's Day of 1756. He was twenty-eight years old and she was sixteen.[18] Lachlan and Sarah had been married a little more than a year when their first child was born in 1757.[19] Following a Scottish tradition of naming boys for their grandfathers, Lachlan and Sarah named their son John in honor of John Mackintosh Mor and called him Jack. Their second son – named Lachlan and called Lachlan Jr. or Lackie – was born in about 1758. Their next son, born in 1759, bore a family name William tracing back to Brigadier William Mackintosh of Borlum, in whose honor Lachlan's older brother had been named. The next was named George in honor of Lachlan's youngest brother. Another son, born in about 1769, was named in honor of Henry Laurens. When the youngest son was named John Hampden, the family had two children with the first name John. Lachlan and Sarah also had two daughters: Esther, born in 1771 and named for Sarah's mother; and Catherine, the youngest child.[20]

Lachlan's older brother William married Mary Jane Mackay. The William McIntoshes, like the Lachlan

McIntoshes, named their sons John, William, Lachlan, and George. William established plantations along the Sapelo and Altamaha rivers and on St. Simon's Island.

In 1758, Lachlan acquired a thousand acres on an island across from Darien on the north branch of the Altamaha River; the tidal flow of the waterways of the island made the property suitable for growing rice. Starting with sixteen slaves, he developed the land into a plantation.[21] Later that year, Lachlan and his brother William acquired a thousand acres on Broughton and Doboy Islands. Eventually acquiring fourteen thousand acres of land and sixty slaves, Lachlan experienced success as a rice planter.

When Lachlan's brother George completed his apprenticeship, Lachlan "brought him back to Georgia and got him appointed Commissary of supplies for the troops in garrison at Frederica" on St. Simon's Island. Lachlan also "instructed him in geometry and surveying and furnished him with books for those purposes" so George could "acquire a more perfect knowledge of his own country and have an opportunity of getting the most valuable lands at this early period for himself" with advice and directions from Lachlan. When George decided on a career as a planter, Lachlan secured loans for George to purchase "a parcel of Negroes." George combined the use of slave labor with "his own industry," Lachlan wrote, "to acquire all the property he ever possessed. Of all these advantages he made the best use and became one the best planters in the state, uniformly ascribing all his successes to [Lachlan]'s steady friendships to him, and always declaring and looking upon [Lachlan] in the light of a father and tried friend rather than a brother."[22] George built a house around 1759 on five hundred acres on the Sapelo River north of Darien. He continued to add acreage to his holdings and became one of the most prosperous planters in Georgia.[23]

Lachlan's sister Ann married Robert Baillie, a Highlander who had immigrated to Darien and who had commanded Fort Barrington on the Altamaha River. After the Independent Company of Foot was disbanded and Fort Barrington was abandoned, Robert and Ann Baillie grew rice on her land at the headwaters of the Sapelo River.[24]

Henry Laurens, who had been Lachlan's mentor in Charleston, acquired nine hundred acres adjacent to Lachlan's property on Broughton Island. As an absentee landowner, Laurens depended on Lachlan to help manage the Broughton Island property. Laurens and Lachlan made other joint investments in various enterprises in coastal Georgia. Lachlan sent his oldest son John to school in Charleston under Laurens' supervision.[25]

Lachlan's father John Mackintosh Mor, who had been a gentleman farmer in Scotland, resumed farming in Georgia and built a home overlooking a saltwater creek. As he grew older, he spent most of his time sitting under a huge oak tree.[26] He died in 1761 at his farm Essick on the Sapelo River.[27] He was buried beside his wife Marjory in the old city cemetery in Darien.[28]

Like their father, Lachlan and George displayed a penchant for leadership in civic life. Lachlan served as tax collector and justice of the peace. Lachlan also supervised an effort to rebuild Fort Frederica, where he had been stationed as a cadet at the time of the Battle of Bloody

Marsh. Lachlan used his surveying skills on road projects and to lay out a new plan of the town of Darien based on Oglethorpe's original concept. George received an appointment as the official surveyor of St. Andrew's Parish. In 1764 and again in 1768 George was elected to serve as a delegate from St. Andrew's Parish to the Commons House of Georgia.[29]

The political factionalism in Georgia that was to plague the McIntosh brothers throughout the Revolutionary era surfaced as early as 1768. When George and his brother-in-law Robert Baillie attempted to take their seats in the Commons House in the autumn of 1768, their election was challenged. Before the controversy was resolved, the royal governor of Georgia dissolved the assembly because the Georgians had supported their fellow colonists in Massachusetts against British policies. When new elections were held, the voters of St. Andrew's Parish did not return either George McIntosh or Robert Baillie to the Commons House. For Baillie, it was the end of his political career.[30]

In 1770, Lachlan McIntosh was elected as a delegate to the Commons House. Once again, the Georgians flexed their political muscle and the royal governor dissolved the assembly. Later, George McIntosh was elected as a delegate from St. Mary's parish, where he had recently purchased property.[31]

On frequent trips to Savannah as a delegate and on other business, George McIntosh associated with the wealthy, socially prominent Houstoun family and became friends with Patrick Houstoun, a son of Sir Patrick Houstoun. George McIntosh fell in love with Ann Priscilla

Houstoun, known as "Nancy," and married her in the spring of 1772; he was thirty-three years old and she was sixteen or seventeen. The marriage of George and Nancy was blessed with a son, John Houstoun McIntosh, called "Jack," on May 1, 1773. Although the boy was named for Nancy's favorite brother, he shared his first name with George's father, the late John Mackintosh Mor; the name had been passed down to one of George's brothers and three of his nephews.[32]

George and Nancy McIntosh and their son lived on their plantation called Rice Hope on the Sapelo River. Her brother Patrick Houstoun lived nearby on Cathead Plantation near Darien. Houstoun served several terms in the Commons House; at any given time at least one of the brothers-in-law was a delegate in the assembly until the American Revolution brought an end to British government in Georgia.[33]

George's brothers William and Lachlan were prominent planters in the neighborhood. George's sister Ann and her husband Robert Baillie also lived on a nearby plantation.

Lachlan McIntosh offered his hospitality to naturalist William Bartram in the spring of 1773, and they continued to correspond throughout their lifetimes. On an expedition to South Georgia and Florida, Bartram delivered a message from Georgia Governor James Wright to Robert Baillie, the husband of Lachlan's sister Ann. Then Bartram sought out Lachlan at his home in Darien, apparently at the suggestion of their mutual friend Henry Laurens.[34]

Georgia historian Edwin J. Cashin has described their meeting:

Of the many people he met and friends he made, with the exception of Mary Lamboll Thomas, William Bartram liked Lachlan McIntosh best. They hit it off from the first. Many years later Bartram's heart filled with sentiment when he recollected that meeting: "When I came up to the door, the friendly man, smiling, and with a grace and dignity peculiar to himself, took me by the hand and accosted me thus, 'Friend Bartram, come under my roof and I desire you to make my house your home as long as convenient to yourself; remember, from this moment that you are part of my family, and on my part I shall endeavor to make it agreeable.'" There were already ten in the McIntosh household so the invitation to Bartram represented a triumph of hospitality over housekeeping. The eight children paraded by to be introduced to their guest... William got along famously with them, and the warmth of their regard drew him to Darien for prolonged visits during his explorations... He especially liked the conversations he had with McIntosh in the evenings, the "improving Philosophic conversation," as he phrased it. The discussions touched on William's favorite theme, the working out of the designs of Providence. He exclaimed, "O my Friend, what a degree of

intellectual enjoyment our nature is susceptible of
when we behold and contemplate the Moral
system impressed on the Human Mind by the
Divine Intelligence."[35]

Bartram invited Jack, the sixteen-year-old son of Sarah
and Lachlan, to accompany him on an expedition. Jack and
Bartram set out from Darien on May 1, 1773. At Augusta
they joined an expedition of at least eighty men, including
contingents of Creek and Cherokee warriors, sent to survey
lands recently ceded to Georgia by the Creek and Cherokee
nations.[36]

When the expedition divided into two teams, Bartram
and Jack accompanied the group that explored the northern
line of the ceded lands. Bartram and Jack rode over rolling
hills to the Tugaloo River and to the Indian town of
Tugaloo in the foothills of the Cherokee mountains. In July,
they reached the junction of the Tugaloo River and the
Savannah River, where two young Indians harpooned
dozens of trout and bream; one trout was two feet long and
weighed about fifteen pounds, Bartram said. The Indian
and white members of the expedition shared a meal of
barbecued fish to celebrate the success of their mission.[37]

On New Year's Day of 1775 a committee formed at Darien
expressed support for the unruly Americans in New
England who challenged British colonial authority. The
committee members asked Lachlan McIntosh to serve as
their leader.[38]

The Darien Committee called for an end to slavery in Georgia. Even though Lachlan owned about sixty slaves and his brother George owned about forty slaves, Lachlan recognized that slavery was untenable. The Darien Committee called slavery "an unnatural practice... founded in injustice and cruelty, and highly dangerous to our liberty (as well as our lives) debasing part of our fellow creatures below men, and corrupting the virtue and morals of the rest, and is laying the basis of that liberty we contend for... upon a very wrong foundation."[39]

Later, the Darien Committee sent the McIntosh brothers William, Lachlan and George as delegates to the Georgia Provincial Congress. On July 4, 1775, the Provincial Congress declared its support for the Continental Congress and established itself as Georgia's revolutionary government. The Georgia Provincial Congress set up a Council of Safety to conduct day-to-day operations of the state government, and George McIntosh served on the Council of Safety. The revolutionaries took Royal Governor James Wright into custody briefly before he escaped onto a British ship in the harbor.[40]

Shortly after Georgia formed a revolutionary government, the Continental Congress authorized a Continental battalion for Georgia. The Georgia Provincial Congress chose officers for the battalion in January of 1776. Again, political factionalism arose. One faction was based in Christ Church Parish in the Savannah area and was considered to be conservative. A competing faction was based in St. John's Parish in the area around Midway and Sunbury, and was considered to be radical. The conservatives nominated Savannah resident Samuel Elbert to command the battalion; Elbert had organized a militia company in 1772, had studied military matters in England, and had been appointed by the Provincial Congress to command the revolutionary state government's militia.[41]

The radicals nominated Button Gwinnett of St. John's Parish. When Gwinnett won the election, the conservatives refused to accept the results. The impasse threatened to destroy the revolutionary government. At this point, both Gwinnett and Elbert withdrew from consideration, allowing the Provisionary Congress to seek a compromise candidate. The compromise candidate turned out to be Lachlan McIntosh, who was not affiliated with either faction and, as a resident of Darien, did not live in either faction's territory. As part of the compromise, Gwinnett was added to Georgia's delegation to the Continental Congress.[42]

Lachlan took command of the Georgia battalion in January of 1776. Lachlan, age forty-eight, held the rank of colonel, and his teenage sons William, Lackie and Jack were subalterns.

Lachlan's fifty-year-old brother William McIntosh led a troop of light horse assigned to protect the Georgia-Florida frontier. A lifetime of experience had prepared William for the assignment. He had participated in an expedition into Florida during the colonial wars when he was a teenager, had served in Oglethorpe's regiment at St. Simon's Island, and had fought in the Battle of Bloody Marsh in 1742.[43]

William's son John McIntosh, who had become an officer in the Continental army in 1775 at age twenty, was promoted to the rank of captain in the 1st Georgia Regiment.[44]

Lachlan's sons William and Lackie would serve throughout the war. Jack, however, went to Jamaica to stay with Lachlan's brother John Mackintosh.[45]

Shortly after Jack left Georgia, Lachlan got some bad news. "I am exceedingly distressed for the ill state of health your uncle and yourself are in," Lachlan wrote Jack. "For God's sake, if this finds you alive, both leave the island immediately. If your uncle is not willing to come, let no consideration detain you on any account. You may find your way to some part of the continent by going to any of the French, Dutch, Danish or Spanish islands, or to St. Augustine, though the last is the worse and most uncertain way. Remember, it was my last charge to you to leave Jamaica whenever you got sick. It was upon that condition I suffered you to go to Jamaica at all."[46]

Both Jack and John survived their bouts of island illnesses, and, despite Lachlan's fatherly distress, Jack remained in Jamaica throughout the war.

Lachlan's younger brother George continued to serve on the Georgia Council of Safety and continued to operate his plantations. In December of 1775 he sent a large shipment of rice from his plantations to a merchant in Savannah, his brother-in-law George Houstoun.

In June of 1776 George McIntosh and his brothers-in-law Robert Baillie and Sir Patrick Houstoun prepared a shipment of rice to a Dutch colony; when George found out in August that the ship had been diverted without his knowledge to British East Florida, he told the Council of

Safety that he had been deceived. Although the Georgia government accepted his explanation, the incident would come back to haunt the McIntosh family.[47]

3
Slanderous and False Insinuations

Lachlan McIntosh and his brothers valued their individual honor and their family honor. When Button Gwinnett and his supporters tried to undermine Lachlan's authority by besmirching his brothers, Lachlan and his brothers fought back as individuals and as a family.

Since the beginning of the American Revolution, Lachlan's older brother William had commanded horsemen defending the southern frontier. For a full year William conducted raids into British East Florida and fended off counter-raids through tangled forests and treacherous swamps. Then the rivalry between Button Gwinnett and Lachlan McIntosh engulfed William McIntosh. Supporters of Gwinnett attempted to discredit Lachlan by attacking William's character. They claimed that William's soldiers had failed to protect Georgians who had ventured into East Florida to raid loyalist settlements. They charged William with abandoning the area south of the Altamaha, although he was acquitted of the charge.

William removed himself from the controversy by requesting a leave of absence. Many of his officers also resigned in protest. At age fifty and beset by illness, William offered valid reasons to quit campaigning in the hot, humid, insect-ridden, fever-inducing environment. Lachlan McIntosh observed "my brother Colonel McIntosh informs me that he is quite worn out with the hardships and fatigue of the service."[1]

Lachlan granted William "leave to retire for a while"[2] and sent Colonel Samuel Elbert to take command on the southern frontier.[3] "I flatter myself your taking the command at Altamaha will bring things to some order there," Lachlan told Elbert. "I am sure it will make me much easier & happier than I have been for some time."[4]

Lachlan McIntosh complained about "the scandalous attempts on the character of my brother William." Lachlan perceived that he himself "was the grand object" of a conspiracy to "pick a hole in my character." In a letter to George Walton, one of Georgia's delegates to the Continental Congress, Lachlan alluded to Button Gwinnett. "I need not inform you of the person or his motives who is at the bottom of the whole;" McIntosh wrote, "all his inventions, industry & nocturnal meetings have only done me honor as he could not make a sufficient party, nor venture to publish one single flaw in my conduct."[5]

"Your enemies," Walton replied, "meant to ruin you indirectly. In my judgment it was intended to tease you into a resignation as they have done your brother."[6]

Controversy around Lachlan McIntosh's oldest brother William had barely begun to fade when more virulent controversy swirled around their youngest brother George. Button Gwinnett lurked in the center of the new controversy.

In late February of 1777, Georgia Council of Safety President Archibald Bulloch died. The Council elected Button Gwinnett as its new president. George McIntosh served on the Council of Safety but was absent for the election because of personal heartbreak. His twenty-one-year-old wife Ann Priscilla – called "Nancy" – died that same day, leaving George McIntosh a widower with two young children: John Houstoun McIntosh, not quite four years old, and Priscilla, a baby. George did attend a meeting called on March 4 for members of the Council to sign Gwinnett's commission. When the commission was handed to George, he refused to sign it.[7]

"I was not present when you were elected," he told Gwinnett. "You would be the last person in the world I would choose."

"By God," Gwinnett responded, "this will be the last day you and I will ever sit together in Council."[8]

Gwinnett's prophecy came true. Gwinnett found a pretense to remove George from office and to heap humiliation on the McIntosh family. Gwinnett based his attack on unproven assertions that George secretly supported British rule. The Continental Congress had intercepted a letter from the governor of British East Florida to the British war secretary saying George had assisted a loyalist merchant in shipping rice to the British subjects in St. Augustine. The letter said George "is compelled to a tacit acquiescence with the distempered times, and is one of the Rebel Congress of Georgia, intentionally to mollify and temporize, and to be of all the service of his power. I am informed his principles are a loyal attachment to the King and Constitution."[9] Congress resolved on January 1, 1777, to inform the Georgia governor and council of the intercepted letter. The resolution also recommended that Georgia authorities "apprehend and secure George McIntosh" and take measures "necessary for the safety of the United States of America."[10] John Hancock, the president of Congress, followed up with instructions dated January 8. Hancock, who did not know George but had served in Congress with Gwinnett, claimed the intercepted letter contained "the most convincing proof of the treasonable conduct of Mr. George McIntosh of your State. This gentleman, it seems, is a member of congress in Georgia and under that character is secretly supporting by every act in his power the designs of the British King and Parliament against us."[11]

Archibald Bulloch, who was president of the Council of Safety when Hancock's letter reached Georgia, "took no notice of it," according to a pamphlet titled *The Case of George M'Intosh,* because Bulloch recognized the McIntosh family's patriotism. An investigation the previous summer, furthermore, had convinced state officials that George McIntosh could not be blamed when rice shipped from his plantation was diverted to British territory without his knowledge or consent.[12]

After Bulloch died and Gwinnett took office, Gwinnett found the resolution of Congress and letter from Hancock. This discovery, the pamphlet said, "was made the pretense for all Mr. McIntosh's persecution, and such cruel and inhuman usage that must alarm every individual."[13] A group of men dragged George McIntosh from his sick bed and "in a harsh, cruel manner, carried him to the dirtiest and most offensive gaol perhaps in the world, with felons, and there fettered in irons." McIntosh's plantations were "taken into possession as if already forfeited and wantonly wasted and abused, by order of the President, without advice or knowledge of his Council or application to the Chief Justice or any other magistrate."[14]

Gwinnett refused to inform McIntosh and his friends of the reason for his arrest, and even refused to tell members of the Council of Safety. Rumors flew around Savannah that "some horrid crime had been *proved* against Mr. McIntosh, which removed all their pity and compassion for him," the pamphlet said. Gwinnett later explained that he expressed his detestation of treason by ordering that McIntosh be put in irons.[15]

McIntosh's friends offered to post £50,000 bail to get him out of jail, but Gwinnett refused the offer. Because many members of the Georgia Council of Safety lived outside Savannah, a couple of days passed before the Council could assemble. Gwinnett presented to the Council the documents from the Continental Congress accusing McIntosh of "treasonable conduct."[16] After reading the documents, the Council ordered that the iron fetters be removed from McIntosh. [17]

Simultaneously with the George McIntosh controversy, Gwinnett made plans for an invasion of Florida without consulting Lachlan McIntosh despite Lachlan's position as commander of Georgia's Continental troops. Gwinnett told General Robert Howe, who coordinated Continental efforts in South Carolina and Georgia, that Lachlan McIntosh had lost the confidence of Georgia's citizens because of the controversy around George McIntosh; Gwinnett recommended that Howe remove Lachlan McIntosh from command in Georgia, but Howe did not follow the recommendation.

On March 19, three days after George McIntosh was arrested, Gwinnett went to Sunbury to make arrangements for an invasion of Florida.

General Howe, declaring that he was not going to participate in an invasion of Florida, announced plans to return to Charleston with the Continental troops that accompanied him. Howe consented to leave Colonel Thomas Sumter's battalion in Georgia, and ordered Sumter to take post at Sunbury.[18]

While Gwinnett met with Howe in Sunbury, the Georgia Council of Safety met in Savannah and allowed George McIntosh to defend himself. He declared that he had never sent any rice out of Georgia other than a cargo destined for Surinam that had been diverted without his knowledge. The Florida governor's false claim that George felt loyalty toward the British king was, George suspected, an act of "designed villainy." Evidence unknown to George supports his suspicion that the Florida governor was lying: in the midst of the controversy, the exiled British governor of Georgia wrote a letter to British officials referring to George McIntosh as "a great rebel."[19] After hearing George's defense, the Council released him on a £20,000 bond and said that he was at liberty to appear before the Continental Congress to answer the charge against him.[20]

Gwinnett's treatment of George McIntosh infuriated Lachlan McIntosh, who felt fiercely protective of his younger brother. Lachlan had taken young George with him to Charleston, where the two of them lived in the same household for eight years before they both returned to their family territory in coastal South Georgia. Personal animosity between Lachlan McIntosh and Gwinnett resulted in antagonism between McIntosh as the commander of Continental troops in Georgia and Gwinnett as leader of the state government and commander of the Georgia militia. Unable to raise enough state militia for his invasion of Florida, Gwinnett finally asked McIntosh in late March for the support of Continental troops.

Although McIntosh called the operation the "Don Quixote expedition to Augustine,"[21] he complied with Gwinnett's request. "Whatever my opinion of the expedition may be," McIntosh told his friend Henry Laurens, "I am resolved to go and do all in my power to forward it and bring it a happy issue."[22]

The Georgia forces reached Sunbury by the middle of April. Sickness took its toll just as it had the year before. McIntosh and Gwinnett argued for weeks over who should be in command of the expedition. The Council of Safety asked both of them to return to Savannah, leaving Colonel Samuel Elbert of the 2nd Georgia Battalion to lead the invasion. McIntosh said he turned the command over to Elbert "for peace' sake."[23]

A request by McIntosh for a hearing before the Council of Safety was "thrown aside," he said, in "an act of injustice unheard of." McIntosh charged that the ill-fated expedition was "first formed to gratify the dangerous ambition of this Man," a pointed reference to Gwinnett. "I fear its consequence," McIntosh wrote, "whereas had he proceeded properly, consulted the officers of the Army in time, and left the prosecution of their business to themselves, it might have had a good effect." McIntosh asked the Georgia House of Assembly for justice "against such oppressions, slanders and falsehoods."[24]

McIntosh later told Henry Laurens, "Ever since Mr. Gwinnett was disappointed in the Brigadier General's commission, which he expected from Congress, himself and party seemed to lose sight of everything else, except to render the army obnoxious and create the utmost confusion and disorder in it; wherein they used the utmost art, invention, and industry on every occasion; and when they found themselves every way disappointed by my circumspection and caution, they fell to personal abuse, slanderous and false insinuations and assertions to my prejudice."[25]

While Lachlan McIntosh and Button Gwinnett struggled to organize an invasion of Florida, George McIntosh gathered affidavits disproving the charge of treason. The charge was based on an incident in June of 1776 when George had shipped rice grown on his plantation. Since he could not trade with any British territory, he had decided to ship the rice to Surinam, a Dutch colony off the Atlantic coast of South America. Without his knowledge or consent, the ship had entered the waters of British East Florida and had procured clearances to protect the shipment from being seized by British warships. Meanwhile, a rumor had arisen that the rice had been unloaded in St. Augustine. Actually, the rice had not gone to either St. Augustine or Surinam and had ended up in Jamaica.[26]

The shipment intended for Surinam had involved a partnership among George McIntosh, Robert Baillie and Sir Patrick Houstoun. Baillie was married to George's sister Ann; Houstoun was a brother of George's wife Ann Priscilla, called Nancy. The three men owned neighboring plantations and were longtime friends as well as in-laws. Their friendship and kinship reached back long before the Revolution and survived the political divisions of Revolutionary Georgia. George McIntosh and his brothers devoted themselves to the patriot cause. Patrick Houstoun's brothers John, James and William were prominent patriots, but Patrick, a former member of Georgia's Royal Council, vacillated between conflicting loyalties; another brother, George Houstoun, supported the patriots early in the war but later leaned toward the loyalists.[27] Baillie, who had served in Oglethorpe's regiment and had commanded the garrison at Fort Barrington in the colonial era, remained loyal to the British government. Whenever the topic of American independence arose, Baillie and George McIntosh "always differed so much that they were (though otherwise on good terms) ever contesting and wrangling on their political sentiments."[28] In 1776 when the American Revolution was in its infancy, Baillie considered moving his family out of Georgia to South America; one of his concerns was that Georgia would be engulfed in an Indian war.[29] Although Georgia patriots disliked Baillie's political stand, they admitted that he was a very honest man.[30]

Baillie gave a detailed statement under oath about the shipment bound for Surinam that was diverted to British East Florida. As plans for the shipment evolved, a trader from Florida named William Panton received permission from the committee of St. Andrew's Parish to get involved with the shipment. Panton and Baillie decided "that the brig should touch at St. Mary's or St. John's [in British East Florida] for a register and clearance in order to secure the vessel from men of war, which was to be concealed from the knowledge of Mr. George McIntosh, knowing that he would not concur in it."[31] When McIntosh later heard that Panton's ship had been seen in the St. John's River in Florida, he suffered "great uneasiness" and said he was "afraid they had been deceived."[32] Witnesses later said that Panton left Florida without unloading the cargo and intended to sell it in the British colony of Tobago. Panton eventually sold the rice in Jamaica, a British colony that was considered enemy territory by American patriots. George McIntosh did not receive any proceeds from the sale.[33]

Under oath, Baillie declared what he knew of McIntosh's political sentiments. "In every conversation the deponent had with Mr. George McIntosh he ever found him to be a warm friend of the American cause: And this deponent further declares that he believes it was owing to Mr. George McIntosh's indefatigable pains that most of the people in this parish signed the Association so early as they did, and was the principal means of keeping up the public meetings and committees. This deponent further says that during Mr. Panton's short stay at his house in June last, political disputes frequently arose between Mr. Panton and Mr. George McIntosh, when the latter always warmly supported the measures of the Continent, and ever appeared uniform in avowing his attachment to the American cause."[34] Baillie then offered a motive for East Florida Governor Patrick Tonyn's damning claim that McIntosh was a friend to the British: Panton had planted the idea with Tonyn to protect McIntosh if, as Panton expected, British forces captured South Carolina and Georgia.[35]

A neighboring planter with solid credentials as a patriot, Raymond Demere, said he would have known if George McIntosh had supplied the enemy with provisions but he knew of "no one instance that has the least tendency towards the support of such an accusation."[36] Calling McIntosh "a warm friend to the American cause," Demere pointed out that "Mr. George McIntosh was among the first of those advocates of this state who early stood forth at the hazard of life and fortune to support the measures of the Continent."[37]

Adding to the affidavits of Baillie and Demere, the manager of McIntosh's plantation swore that the plantation had not sent any rice or other provisions out of Georgia except the one shipment intended to go to Surinam.[38]

While George McIntosh gathered evidence to prove himself innocent of treason, Georgia's invasion of Florida proceeded fitfully. After Lachlan McIntosh returned to

Savannah, Colonel Samuel Elbert commanded the Continental troops at Sunbury. Elbert loaded his men on transports escorted by two sloops and three row galleys and, on May 1, floated down the inland waterway from Sunbury toward Florida. Meanwhile, a mounted force under Colonel John Baker rode southward, planning to rendezvous with Elbert's men at the mouth of the St. John's River. For Baker's men, crossing the Altamaha was difficult and time-consuming because the river had risen to flood stage. When they finally got across the Altamaha, Indians attacked their camp and wounded two soldiers. Baker's men spent the rest of the day chasing the Indians without success. The next day they resumed their trek southward, where the rain-swollen Satilla and St. Mary's Rivers awaited them. They managed to reach the rendezvous point according to schedule on May 12 and discovered that Elbert's flotilla had not yet arrived.[39]

Problems with Georgia's invasion of Florida damaged the prestige of the man who proposed the invasion, Button Gwinnett. When a new Georgia constitution called for a governor rather than a president as chief of state, Gwinnett ran for the post but was defeated.

The assembly under the new constitution held hearings on Gwinnett's conduct during preparations for the invasion. As the hearings concluded, Lachlan McIntosh accosted Gwinnett.

"You," McIntosh told Gwinnett, "are a scoundrel and lying rascal!"[40]

Late in the evening of Thursday, May 15, 1777, McIntosh received a written challenge from Gwinnett. Because McIntosh had called him a scoundrel in public conversation, Gwinnett desired that McIntosh "would give satisfaction for it as a gentleman, before sunrise next morning in Sir James Wright's pasture, behind Colonel Martin's house."[41]

McIntosh answered that he would meet Gwinnett with a pair of dueling pistols. He agreed to arrive at Wright's pasture before sunrise, "although the hour is rather earlier than my usual."[42]

McIntosh kept his promise to arrive before sunrise and was waiting in the pasture when Gwinnett arrived. They saluted one another politely but avoided any conversation other than making arrangements for the duel. McIntosh produced the dueling pistols and showed that each was loaded with only a single ball.

Spectators appeared at Wright's pasture, just outside of Savannah on the road to Thunderbolt. The duelists withdrew down a slight incline in the pasture and chose a place for the duel. In negotiations over how far apart the duelists would be when they exchanged fire, Gwinnett said "Whatever distance the General pleases." McIntosh said, "I believe eight or ten feet will be sufficient." Assistants, called "seconds" in dueling terminology, asked to add one more step to the measurement.

The seconds suggested that the duelists turn back to back. McIntosh replied "By no means. Let us see what we are about."[43] The duelists took their stands facing one another.

McIntosh and Gwinnett shot at one another at nearly the same time.

Gwinnett fell to the ground with a wound above the knee and said his thigh was broken.

McIntosh remained standing despite a wound through the thick of his thigh. He asked, "Have you had enough? Or are you for another shot?"

The seconds objected to another shot, declaring that both duelists had "behaved like gentlemen and men of honor."[44]

McIntosh walked across the dueling ground to Gwinnett and shook his hand. Then McIntosh smashed his pistol against a tree, breaking the stock.[45] Gwinnett and McIntosh left the dueling field for their homes.

"Mr. Gwinnett was brought in, the weather extreme hot, a mortification came on – he languished from that morning (Friday) till Monday morning following, and expired," lamented Gwinnett's friend, neighbor, political ally and fellow signer of the Declaration of Independence Lyman Hall. "O Liberty! Why do you suffer so many of your faithful sons, your warmest votaries to fall at your shrine! Alas my friend! My friend!"[46]

Official reaction to the duel awaited the next meeting of the Georgia Assembly, when McIntosh was arrested for killing Gwinnett. McIntosh was acquitted at trial, but that did not quell a political firestorm raging around him.[47]

On June 3, eighteen days after he had been wounded in the duel, McIntosh said he had "recovered so well that in a few days I expect to resume the exercise of my duty as usual."[48]

McIntosh sent Henry Laurens depositions of witnesses to "the late affair between the unfortunate Mr. Gwinnett and myself, to prevent misrepresentations which I have reason to expect from the unremitting although undeserved malice of the relics of the party." In the immediate aftermath, while both Gwinnett and McIntosh were still alive, the duel "seemed to give general satisfaction throughout the state to all parties, as if our unhappy divisions were thereby at an end." Gwinnett's death, "evidently owing to the unskillfulness of the doctor, appeared to make no alteration in the mind of anyone except myself, who was partly the unfortunate but innocent instrument of it." Gwinnett's widow "publicly declared me innocent and altogether blameless, and often enquired after my health."[49]

In his letter to Laurens, McIntosh conjectured that the duel had arisen from a conspiracy by the Gwinnet faction:

> Knowing my declared aversion, from principle, to private quarrels and dueling, until at length my best friends were astonished at my forbearance, and my enemies construed it into a meaning, which made them prompt the unfortunate man to his own destruction, though it was intended to bring me into this dilemma: if I refused the challenge, on any pretense, they would immediately cry out, "How unworthy he is to hold his commission!" although I have on all occasions exposed myself more than any other soldier

> under my command in defense of the state…
> And, if I accepted it and fell, they would get
> rid of me, who, at all times, exposed publicly
> their designs against the freedom, peace and
> order of the state; or have an opportunity of
> plaguing me if that should be the fate of my
> antagonist.[50]

As soon as the shock of the duel subsided, the Gwinnett faction renewed attempts to undermine McIntosh. Gwinnett's widow switched from declaring McIntosh blameless to calling him "a very traitor, it would fill volumes to relate his treacherous villainy."[51] She joined a chorus of Georgians in demanding that McIntosh be removed from command, "which will in some measure satisfy a disconsolate widow and daughter."[52]

While politicians in Savannah weighed the wisdom of invading Florida, the men actually involved in the invasion were fighting for their lives. Colonel Thomas Brown's Florida Rangers discovered the camp of Colonel John Baker's invasion force on May 14. That night, Brown's Indian allies stole forty of Baker's horses. When morning came, Baker followed the tracks for four miles and found the horses hobbled beside a swamp. Baker believed the Indians were waiting in ambush in the swamp. He left a party of men in plain sight to divert the Indians and sent two other parties to cut the hobbles and drive the horses away from the swamp. When his tactic succeeded, the

Indians came out of ambush and pursued Baker's men for a mile. Although Baker's men outnumbered the Indians sixty to fifteen, Baker could not make his men stop and face the Indians in battle. During the pursuit, a young Indian was killed and two of Baker's men were wounded. The Indians called off the chase and burned the woods so that they could not be tracked. Baker's men scalped and mutilated the dead Indian.[53]

Because the British knew the location of his camp, Baker moved inland. The British intercepted his line of march and prepared for battle. The British forces totaled about two hundred, while Baker had 150 to 180 horsemen. On May 17, Thomas Brown's loyalists and allied Indians ambushed the Americans at Thomas Creek, which flows into the Nassau River. The Americans attempted to retreat but were cut off by a hundred regular British soldiers commanded by Mark Prevost. The Americans fled through the swamp, and Baker narrowly escaped capture. Three Americans were killed, nine wounded and thirty-one captured. As the Americans moved toward Georgia, one man drowned in the Satilla River.[54]

On May 18, Colonel Samuel Elbert's flotilla stopped at Amelia Island to gather provisions for the invasion force. Loyalists killed a lieutenant and badly wounded two men who were rounding up cattle and pigs. In retaliation, Elbert ordered that every house on Amelia be burned and all the livestock killed. Elbert's forces also seized at least seven slaves from plantations on Amelia.

While Elbert was at Amelia Island, fifteen of Baker's men arrived and told of their defeat. Three more of Baker's men arrived a few days later and reported that Indians had killed five of the Americans who had been taken prisoner in the battle at Thomas Creek.

Elbert attempted to continue the invasion down the inland waterway, but the flotilla was unable to navigate the narrow passage between Amelia Island and the mainland despite six days of effort. The invasion force had dwindled to about three hundred men healthy enough to fight. The men were running out of provisions and subsisted on rice for five days. With British forces guarding the river crossings and British vessels patrolling the coast, Elbert decided to withdraw. Most of the force embarked on the flotilla to return northward, while a hundred men marched overland, destroying settlements and farms along the way.[55]

The famished men of Georgia's invasion force reached Fort Howe on the Altamaha River on June 9 and proceeded to Darien the next day. At Darien, Elbert ordered Colonel Screven of the 3rd Regiment to take several hundred men to the Satilla to protect Georgians who were driving cattle out of the disputed land. As soon as the Georgians succeeded in driving about a thousand cattle north of the Altamaha, Screven's regiment returned to Fort Howe.[56]

Georgia officials then adopted a defensive strategy. In early June the assembly approved two battalions of minute men to defend the frontier, and General Lachlan McIntosh renewed recruiting efforts to bring the Continental regiments to full strength. To encourage the officers doing the recruiting, he ordered numerous promotions. As a result, his nephew John McIntosh rose from captain to major of the 1st Battalion.[57] Lachlan's son William was promoted to captain.[58]

During the summer in coastal Georgia, many of the soldiers became ill, so General McIntosh moved most of them inland to healthier locations with better water, leaving a detachment at Sunbury. The 2nd Regiment under Colonel Elbert was stationed on the Savannah River and the 3rd Regiment under Colonel Screven was stationed on the Ogeechee River.

McIntosh's feud and duel with Button Gwinnett complicated his relationship with Colonel John Baker. When petitions for removing McIntosh from command were circulated after the duel, Baker reportedly told his whole regiment to sign. When McIntosh reassigned Baker's regiment of light horse from the western frontier to the southern frontier, the orders were not carried out. Baker's men were dispirited because they had lost their horses and they had not been paid for their military service. The officers complained that their financial accounts had not been certified. Feeling that he had been unjustly criticized, Baker resigned.

The Georgia government tried to go over McIntosh's head by giving Elbert command of the Continental troops on the western frontier, but Elbert abided by the chain of command that placed McIntosh in charge of all Continental troops in Georgia.

Ongoing political feuds kept alive the accusation of treason against George McIntosh. "Mr. McIntosh is among the very few in Georgia whose patriotism was divested of every view of profit or parade, as he neither sought or would accept any office for advantage," said a pamphlet offering his point of view. "The truth is, Mr. McIntosh, who had no lucrative motives himself, ever opposed those who had no other, and who had designs against the liberties of their country, which is solely the cause of his present persecution."[59]

The Georgia House of Assembly resolved on June 5, 1777, to send George McIntosh under a strong guard to the Continental Congress for trial.[60] The June 5 resolution differed greatly from the Council of Safety's resolution the previous March that if McIntosh expressed a "desire" to appear before Congress he would be "at liberty to do so."[61] In the McIntosh tradition of upholding personal and family honor, a pro-McIntosh pamphlet said "it is a worse punishment than death itself to a man of character or any reputation to be carried with infamy, like a felon, as a spectacle, 1000 miles through the States of the Continent."[62] McIntosh argued that legal cases should be tried in courts rather than before Congress. "Congress does not pretend to act as a judicial court," pointed out the pamphlet *The Case of George M'Intosh*. "These matters they leave to the local laws of the particular states." The Congressional resolution merely recommended that Georgia officials take McIntosh into custody and take any action that they saw fit; the resolution did not call for McIntosh to be brought before Congress.[63]

Contacting Lachlan McIntosh and others who had provided security to have George released on bond, Governor John Adam Treutlen threatened to have the bond forfeited unless they produced him. When George reported to Savannah on June 16, he felt that he had fulfilled the terms of the bond.

While George continued to ask for a trial in Georgia, Treutlen and the council refused to meet with him. George then asked to be treated as a gentleman on his journey to Philadelphia to represent himself before Congress. The council granted his request and entered it into the council's minutes but, at a later meeting, the council withdrew its approval of his request and restored its order that he be sent to Congress under a strong guard.

George responded to the council's surprise decision by secretly leaving Savannah. State officials insinuated that he must be guilty because he had absconded; they claimed that he had taken refuge in St. Augustine in British East Florida. George, however, remained in Georgia and continued to profess his innocence. "They have not proved one single crime against me with all their art and malice," he told a friend in a letter dated July 4, "and they are afraid to give me a fair hearing, either before the Legislature, Executive, or Judicial Departments; well knowing and convinced that I can clear myself of everything they lay to my charge."[64]

When George arrived at his home near Darien, he discovered that men from St. John's Parish who said they were acting on the governor's orders had ransacked his plantation. The men had "taken possession of my estate," George wrote to his friend, "destroyed all my crops on the ground by turning their horses into it, killed and drove off my stock of every kind, broke open my house, barn and cellar, plundered and carried off everything of value they could find, and still continue there committing every waste in their power." His "faithful and trusty overseer" had been banished from his plantation.[65] Then George received more horrendous news: "I am just informed one of my trusty Negroes upon my indigo plantation was cruelly whipped until he died in the rope because the poor fellow could not tell where I was."[66]

The pillaging left George "without house or home, in my native country, and what property I have been collecting in an honest way, these twenty years past, arbitrarily and unjustly taken from me, without any form of trial."[67]

The men from St. John's also seized the slaves and overseers from William McIntosh, who was George's oldest brother, and from James Spalding, the husband of William's daughter Margery. Without their slaves, the McIntosh and Spalding planters could not harvest their fine crop of indigo. Many of the friends and neighbors of the McIntosh family became destitute and found subsistence on the oyster banks. Once-prosperous planters pondered abandoning their property and relocating to another state where citizens were not subjected to the injustices George McIntosh suffered.[68]

George lost his home and property within six months of the death of his wife. He fretted over the prospects of his four-year-old son John Houstoun McIntosh and his baby daughter Priscilla, "my poor unfortunate and helpless children made beggars, and myself wandering from place to place through the woods like a vagabond and an outlaw." He asked his friend to excuse the sloppiness of his handwriting as he wrote the letter "upon my knee, and under a tree."[69] After suffering from poor health for several months, his tribulations reduced him to "a mere skeleton, worn off his legs and hardly able to stand." In addition to his physical plight, he suffered from an emotional condition in which he "is grown indifferent to his family, property and everything else."[70]

Lachlan McIntosh said his brother George "is now hunted through the woods and swamps like a partridge" in a letter to a friend. "His present situation is truly deplorable, hiding himself from camp to camp in the swamps, his children neglected, his crops gone, part of his slaves in custody and part in the woods, his stock &c destroyed. Surely some retaliation should be made for his losses though none can be made for such usage to an innocent man."[71]

In late July, George made plans for a trip to Philadelphia, where Congress was meeting. He appointed John Wereat and his brother Lachlan as his attorneys in his absence.[72] As he was preparing to leave, a state official delivered a note ordering George to turn himself in immediately to the provost marshal. "Such a sudden and unexpected note surprised me much," George wrote. He asked around town and discovered that the Council of Safety "had resolved in a private manner" to transport him to Philadelphia "in the most ignominious manner they could" under a twenty-man guard. The guards were commanded by "one Colonel Ferrel, a man of infamous character" who "intended carrying me in irons through the continent."[73]

George foiled the plot by immediately setting off from Savannah to Philadelphia "without waiting to send for my clothes, which were 50 miles out of town." George traveled with a man named Andrew Donaldson who also had plans to go to Philadelphia. Jonathan Bryan accompanied Donaldson and McIntosh the first forty miles of the trip.[74]

"I take the liberty to inform you that I am on my way to Philadelphia," McIntosh wrote Governor Treutlen on July 18 "because I think *there* I shall find justice." Noting that Treutlen had sworn to uphold the Georgia constitution, McIntosh said "I would like to know under what article of this Constitution my present cruel persecution is justified." McIntosh asked that "my property may not be wantonly wasted or destroyed before I am convicted of any crime." He assured Treutlen that "one thousand pounds would not pay the damage already done to my two plantations in St. Andrew's parish."[75]

Georgia officials then sent the guards commanded by Colonel Ferrel in pursuit of McIntosh. Governor Treutlen declared that McIntosh had "skulked off like a guilty thing."[76] When the pursuers reached Charlotte, North Carolina, they learned that McIntosh had passed through several days earlier. Colonel Ferrel ordered Captain Nash to pursue McIntosh "with all speed" and "to press men and horses." Ferrel ordered Nash to offer McIntosh "no kind of indulgence but, on the contrary, to use [McIntosh] in a very rough and harsh manner."[77]

Captain Nash replied, "Sir, in obedience to your orders, I will pursue Mr. McIntosh but my treatment to that gentleman when I come up with him must be left to me."[78]

Donaldson and McIntosh "proceeded on our journey without any interruption through South and North Carolina until the 6th of August, we then being within 16 miles of Virginia. Captain Nash of the 3rd Georgia Battalion came up with us with three or four others." After riding four or five miles together, Nash showed McIntosh the official order requiring the guard to escort McIntosh to Philadelphia. "Sir," Nash said, "I am sorry that I should be sent upon such a disagreeable errand, but you know I must obey my superior officers."[79]

During the time that George McIntosh was traveling to Philadelphia, Lachlan McIntosh and John Wereat tried to carry out their duties as his attorneys. When slaves were stolen from his plantation, the attorneys convinced a judge to order that the slaves be found and returned. The state legislature, however, said that the slaves had not been stolen but rather had been seized legally. The governor and council reprimanded the judge "for having dared to issue his warrant" and "superceded" it by an order that the slaves not be returned. "No man, after this, can pretend to say that law, justice, or equity have any existence in the State of Georgia, but that cruelty, tyranny, and oppression are established upon their ruin," wrote Lachlan McIntosh and Wereat.[80]

When George McIntosh arrived in Philadelphia on August 20, he produced a letter of support from Henry Laurens, in whose household George and Lachlan had lived for several years when they were young. Congress appointed a three-member committee to examine the documents relating to George McIntosh's case. After only one day of deliberation, the committee found no reason to detain McIntosh.[81]

The case drew the attention of South Carolinian William Henry Drayton, who called the Georgia government "a disgrace and detriment to the American cause" because of "circumstances of tyranny, and total disregard to the most valuable rights of the people, that not only ought to alarm every honest and sensible man in Georgia, but fill such with indignation" toward state officials. Under the management of the Georgia government, "the life and liberty of the subjects are in the greatest danger," Drayton said, "or we would not, among many other enormities, have seen George McIntosh, Esquire, who I consider as an abused gentleman, arbitrarily ordered into a distant state, to be tried by those who have no such jurisdiction in such a case."[82]

While George McIntosh defended the family honor in Philadelphia, his older brother Lachlan worked to protect his own reputation and his military career in the turmoil following his duel with Button Gwinnett. Lachlan's old friend and business partner Henry Laurens came to his aid. Laurens, who held a powerful position in the Continental

Congress, arranged for Lachlan to report to General George Washington for reassignment. Washington issued the order reassigning Lachlan on August 6 and, when the order arrived in Georgia, Colonel Samuel Elbert assumed command of Continental forces in Georgia. With George released and Lachlan reassigned, the brothers set out in opposite directions, Lachlan going from Georgia to Washington's army in Pennsylvania and George going from Philadelphia to Georgia. By the time George got home, he was not only debilitated by physical and emotional injuries inflicted by his imprisonment and inquisition but also bereft of his older brother and protector Lachlan. Presumably his Houstoun in-laws took care of George's four-year-old son and months-old daughter and may have offered refuge to George as well.[83]

Lachlan and his son Lackie traveled together from Georgia through South Carolina and North Carolina in the autumn of 1777. In Virginia, Lachlan left Lackie to be inoculated against smallpox.[84]

While Lachlan was on his way to join Washington's army, Washington was engaged in fierce fighting at Brandywine on September 11 and Germantown on October 4. British forces occupied Philadelphia and constructed strong fortifications around the city. During the British occupation of Philadelphia, the town of York, Pennsylvania, served as the temporary seat of the United States government. With members of the Continental Congress scattered before the British onslaught, the responsibilities of Congress fell on its president, Henry

Laurens, and a few clerks. Laurens often stayed up until midnight working on government business.[85]

Washington moved his army into position to hold the British army in check. He chose a defensible location twenty miles from Philadelphia and encamped for the winter at Valley Forge. Lachlan McIntosh reported for duty at Valley Forge on December 17, 1777.

4

Great Worth and Merit

From the moment he took command of Continental forces, Lachlan McIntosh had maintained correspondence with George Washington. While serving at Valley Forge together they developed a sense of camaraderie. Not only were they both Continental generals, but in civilian life both of them were planters and both of them had worked as surveyors. They also had a common friend in high places: Henry Laurens not only had been a business partner with McIntosh for decades but also became Washington's most powerful supporter in Congress. Washington consistently supported McIntosh and always spoke highly of him. Washington described McIntosh as "an officer of great worth and merit" and praised his "firm disposition and equal justice; his assiduity and good understanding."[1] Their friendship lasted throughout the rest of their lives.

At Valley Forge, Washington appointed McIntosh to take command of the North Carolina brigade, which had been without a general since Francis Nash died after a cannon ball broke his thigh at Germantown. Like the other American soldiers at Valley Forge, the North Carolina brigade endured harsh wintry weather in rough huts and ragged tents. The soldiers suffered from scarcity of food, clothing and other provisions. Officially, the North Carolina brigade mustered 2,700 troops, but only 928 were counted at Valley Forge in December and half of them were unfit for duty: 327 were sick and 164 lacked adequate clothing. Faced with this situation, McIntosh asked the "walking sick" to help build huts. As the winter progressed through January and February, the reports grew more dismal: an average of eighty-eight men sick in camp, 299 sick in hospitals and 199 unfit for duty because clothing was not supplied. For a while, the brigade's medical corps dwindled to one doctor and one assistant. McIntosh appealed to North Carolina Governor Richard Caswell to help the brigade, but the state could not overcome financial and logistical problems. Despite the hardships, the desertion rate in the North Carolina brigade was the lowest in the American army at Valley Forge.[2]

In early 1778, Washington used the wintertime break in fighting to mold a motley assembly of men into an organized army. His efforts were enhanced by Friedrich von Steuben, an experienced European military officer who called himself Baron de Steuben and would become known as the Drillmaster of Valley Forge. On his way to Valley Forge, Steuben stopped in York to meet Henry Laurens, the president of the Continental Congress. Laurens suggested that Steuben seek out his son John, an aide on Washington's staff. Henry explained that John not only could speak Steuben's language but also shared many interests with Steuben, including military strategy, political issues, philosophy, literature and social enlightenment. As his father predicted, John Laurens took a strong liking to Steuben as soon as Steuben arrived at Valley Forge. The long-standing relationship between the McIntosh family and the Laurens family may have helped Lackie McIntosh receive an assignment as an aide to Steuben. A coincidence of timing also may have helped; after a stopover in Virginia to be inoculated against smallpox, Lackie had arrived at Valley Forge on February 13, just eleven days before Steuben arrived.[3]

Conditions at Valley Forge were somewhat better for officers than for common soldiers. Many of the officers' wives joined them for the winter and invited Steuben and other high-ranking officers to refined dinner parties. Seeing that his aides like Lackie had fewer social opportunities, Steuben threw a party just for them and their friends; the aides enjoyed a night of feasting, singing and imbibing several rounds of potent drinks.[4]

Washington worked ceaselessly to improve the organization of the army, particularly the departments responsible for food, clothing and other provisions. Anticipating resumption of warfare as winter waned, Washington concentrated on recruitment efforts to bring his army to fighting strength. Washington approved Lachlan McIntosh's suggestion to consolidate the North Carolina brigade from nine regiments into three battalions, resulting in a surplus of former regimental officers who could be sent on recruitment missions. The army at Valley Forge grew from about four thousand fit for duty in February to more than eleven thousand fit for duty in early May.

Lachlan McIntosh played in role in securing beef for the soldiers at Valley Forge. Washington asked McIntosh to provide safe passage for a herd of five hundred cattle promising much-needed nourishment for the soldiers.

Receiving intelligence that "a considerable number of the enemy, both horse and foot" had gathered to intercept the cattle drive, Washington ordered McIntosh "immediately to cross the Schuylkill with the detachment of your command and endeavor to discover the number, situation and intention of the enemy." Realizing that McIntosh was not familiar with the Pennsylvania countryside, Washington assured him that "Colonel Nagle, who will be with you, knows the country well and will provide a number of good officers likewise well acquainted with it," and added, "There is a gentleman on the other side of the river, Colonel Corry, perfectly acquainted with every road. Send to him and he will attend you instantly, and will be very useful to you."[5]

Washington advised McIntosh, "It will be proper to send an officer to meet the cattle and to order them to be kept pretty high up and by observing the route of the enemy it will be easy to keep between them and the cattle. If you should find their numbers and situation such that you can attack them to advantage, I expect that you will do it, but that I will leave to your judgement and the intelligence you shall receive."[6] McIntosh succeeded in locating the herd and escorting it to safety without engaging in combat, although he sensed hostility among residents along the route.[7]

For McIntosh's next assignment, Washington asked him to inspect the military hospitals in Pennsylvania and New Jersey. McIntosh spent several weeks visiting the hospitals and reporting to Washington on conditions he found.[8]

Washington's confidence in McIntosh rose after each assignment and, in May of 1778, Washington assigned the greatest responsibility in McIntosh's career: commander of the Western Department. Congress had approved an expedition against the British western headquarters at Fort Detroit and authorized the formation of two regiments for the expedition. On the same day, Congress had accepted the resignation of the commander of the Western Department and asked Washington to appoint a replacement. Washington, whose vision of the future of the United States included western expansion, wanted a commander who could remain neutral among competing claims by land companies, speculators, colonizers and state officials from Pennsylvania and Virginia.[9] "After much consideration," Washington informed the president of the Continental Congress, "I have appointed General McIntosh to command at Fort Pitt and in the Western Country." Knowing that McIntosh would face feuding factions, Washington wished that the task could be "more agreeable" but felt that McIntosh had an advantage in "being a stranger to all parties in that quarter." While showing confidence in McIntosh's qualifications for an independent command, Washington expressed "much reluctance" in detaching McIntosh from the main army because "his services here are and will be materially wanted."[10] Washington wrote to a regimental commander at Fort Pitt that "I have great expectations" for McIntosh based on "his prudence, good sense and knowledge of negotiation in Indian affairs, which

I imagine he has been conversant with during his long residence in Carolina and Georgia."[11]

Washington informed McIntosh of his assignment in a letter dated May 26, 1778. "I am induced, but not without reluctance, from the sense I entertain of your merit, to nominate you, as an officer well qualified from a variety of considerations," Washington wrote. "I have only to add, that I shall be happy to hear from you, as often as opportunity will permit, and my warmest wishes, that your services may be honorable to yourself and approved by your country."[12]

Lackie also transferred from Valley Forge to the Western Department. Lackie's "stay in camp this winter for improving himself in discipline is approved," Washington wrote, "and while he remains with the General he is to act as brigade inspector to the troops under his command."[13] Lachlan later appointed Lackie to serve as the Deputy Adjutant General for the Western Department.[14]

General Lachlan McIntosh and Captain Lackie McIntosh headed west together. In late May they arrived at York, Pennsylvania, where Congress was meeting. Lachlan had an opportunity to visit his longtime friend and business partner Henry Laurens.

At York, Lachlan discovered that the Board of War had not recruited the two regiments that Congress had authorized for the expedition against Fort Detroit and also had not secured supplies for the expedition.

Since part of the 13th Virginia Regiment was already at the Western Department's headquarters at Fort Pitt, General Washington designated the entire regiment to serve in the expedition; the commander of the regiment, Colonel John Gibson, knew the language and culture of the Indians on the western frontier. Although Washington needed as much strength as possible in his own army at Valley Forge, he also ordered the 8th Pennsylvania Regiment under Colonel Daniel Brodhead to participate in the expedition. The assignment of regiments from both Virginia and Pennsylvania fit into American plans to prevent either Virginia or Pennsylvania from claiming ownership of the western territory due to military conquest by either of the states alone. Other troops joined the expedition, including Colonel George Morgan, the Indian Agent for the Middle Department who also was a land speculator eyeing the Ohio Valley.[15]

Congress appropriated nearly $933,000 for provisions, and authorized a force of three thousand Continental troops and up to 2,5000 Virginia militia. Virginia authorities, however, failed to provide the militia force and would not send the supplies requested by Congress. Plans for the expedition ground to a halt as the month of June came to an end.[16]

Indians attacked settlements in western Pennsylvania in mid-July, throwing settlers into a panic across the western colonial frontier; McIntosh detached the 13th Virginia Regiment to protect the settlements.

The expedition against Fort Detroit finally got underway, crossing the mountains west of York and

marching to the fork of the Ohio River. McIntosh reached
the Western Department headquarters at Fort Pitt on
August 6. By then, Congress had decided to abandon the
expedition against Fort Detroit. His new orders from
Congress were to attack the Indian towns in western
Pennsylvania.[17]

Logistical problems bogged down preparations for
attacking the Indian towns. The Virginia Council
countermanded McIntosh's order to raise militia units for
his expedition. Food for the army was lost or spoiled during
transport across the mountains; McIntosh's queries into the
losses created hard feelings in the supply corps. Local
farmers claimed they could not spare any provisions for the
army or grain for its pack-horses and cattle because they
barely had enough to provide for their own families and
livestock.[18]

While serving in the West, McIntosh remained concerned
about affairs in Georgia. In August he composed two drafts
of a letter "intended to be sent from Pittsburgh by my son
Lackie to Governor Houstoun of Georgia." He said "I could
not help discharging my duty" to his home state "for if love
of a particular spot of ground is a public virtue, I think I
may claim it equal to any person that ever lived; if it is a
vice, no one upon Earth is more criminal than myself."
Mentioning "the contemptibleness" of the political faction
that had caused him to transfer out of his home state and
had persecuted his brother George, he wrote "I heartily
rejoice that Georgia has lately changed its plan of men and

measures." He proposed recruiting families from the region around Pittsburgh to take "grants from Georgia for any lands they settled and improved" in territory claimed by Georgia because "I know our state is weak and has not men enough even for the east side of it, much less to spare any" for settling the frontier.[19]

Shortly after arriving at Fort Pitt, McIntosh negotiated an alliance with the Delaware tribe. The Delaware agreed to help the Americans fight the British, and the Americans promised to provide protection, including a military post to defend their territory. The Americans not only offered trading privileges but also guaranteed that the Delaware would keep their land forever.[20]

The Delaware and the Americans agreed that "should it be for the future found conducive to the mutual interest of both parties to invite any other tribes who have been friends to the interests of the United States to join the present confederation [the United States] and to form a state whereof the Delaware nation shall be the head and have a representative in Congress."[21]

The Treaty of Fort Pitt, concluded in mid-September, became the first Indian treaty signed in the name of the United States. This first treaty, like so many to follow, exploited the Indians who trusted the United States. "There never was a conference with the Indians so improperly or villainously conducted," declared George Morgan, a white official who advocated respect for Indian nations.[22] Delaware leaders claimed that the text of the treaty did not match the translation they heard during the negotiations. "I have now looked over the articles of the treaty and they are wrote down false," said a leader named Killbuck, "and as I did not understand the interpreter what he spoke I could not contradict his interpretation."[23] The Delaware thought they had been offered statehood, for instance, but the text of the treaty contained the subtle disclaimer "nothing contained in this article to be conclusive until it meets with the approbation of Congress."[24]

The text of the treaty also said that a fort in Delaware territory would protect women, children and old people "whilst their warriors are engaged against the common enemy,"[25] implying an obligation to serve in the American army that the Delaware did not accept. "General McIntosh and the Commissioners of Congress put a war belt and tomahawk into the hands of the Delaware Nation and induced some of their chiefs to sign certain writings, which to them were perfectly unintelligible and which they have since found were falsely interpreted to them and contained declarations and engagements they never intended to make or enter into," Killbuck later complained to Congress. "The said Delaware nation have since returned the said tomahawk and belt into the hands of the agent for the United States and desired him to bury them for they have caused great confusion among us."[26]

After the treaty was signed, McIntosh recognized the assistance of a Delaware leader named White Eyes by promoting him from captain to lieutenant colonel on September 21, 1778. McIntosh praised the leader's "solid and sound judgement, his steady and unalterable attachment to the interests of the United States and humanity, amidst the general disaffection, prejudice, and corruption of his countrymen." Because White Eyes was "likely to be of considerable service by his knowledge, understanding, and influence," McIntosh gave White Eyes "the title of Lieutenant Colonel of all the Indian Nations between the rivers Ohio, Mississippi and the Lakes."[27]

Shortly after negotiating the Treaty of Fort Pitt, White Eyes died under mysterious circumstances. His death was attributed to small pox, although no one else had small pox at that time and place. Years later the story arose that White Eyes had been murdered by white people described as renegades who quickly buried his body and took a vow of secrecy.[28]

Enlarging on ideas outlined in the Treaty of Fort Pitt, McIntosh decided to build a series of forts as bases for operations inside Indian territory. The forts would extend along the route toward Detroit, which would be helpful if Congress again authorized an expedition against the western British headquarters at Fort Detroit.[29] The plan got underway in the autumn of 1778 when McIntosh marched thirty miles west of Fort Pitt to a bluff over the Ohio River about a mile below the junction with Beaver River. Construction of Fort McIntosh atop the bluff marked two historic milestones: first, McIntosh's army of more than 1,300 troops was the largest force ever gathered on the western side of the Appalachians throughout the course of the Revolution and, second, the United States established its first military post on the northern side of the Ohio River, which until then had been Indian territory. The engineer officer in the Western Department designed Fort McIntosh in the shape of a four-pointed star with bastions projecting from the points. McIntosh transferred the headquarters from Fort Pitt to Fort McIntosh on October 8.[30]

With Fort McIntosh firmly established, McIntosh attempted to implement his plan to construct another fort farther west. The second fort would fulfill the treaty obligation to establish a defensive post in Delaware tribal territory. His grand plan continued to be undermined by mundane matters of supplies and provisions for the Western Department. The orderly book for October 22, 1778, noted that McIntosh had "unsuccessfully endeavored to engage the wholesome and useful article of beer for the soldiers of this Department on reasonable terms" and had ceased dealing with brewer Agnus Labatt for "extorting unmercifully upon the soldiers upon all occasions."[31]

McIntosh asked the magistrates of Westmoreland County, Pennsylvania, to find a way to provide feed for horses and cattle. Addressing the political problems plaguing the expedition, he wrote, "I have the more reason to expect your assistance in this, as the people of Virginia think me partial to your state, for allowing all your militia to remain home at this time, to defend your own frontiers… whoever attempts to foment or revive these old jealousies, which I could wish to be buried in oblivion, have some sinister designs of their own and are no friends to their country."[32]

Leaving 150 men at Fort McIntosh, the remaining 1,200 men marched westward on November 4. The march was slowed by lack of supplies for the men and lack of forage for the horses in the harsh climate of western Pennsylvania in late autumn. Two soldiers who went out to hunt on November 7 were killed and scalped. In response to the two deaths, McIntosh severely punished soldiers who hunted or fired guns, traded with Indians, or left camp without permission. Such discipline angered the soldiers, who counted on hunting to augment the army's meager supplies.[33]

McIntosh reported the pack horses procured for the expedition were unfit for the task. Since each extra day on the trail required additional food for the men and the animals, the slow pace would have serious consequences. Harsh weather afflicted the marchers late on the afternoon of November 10 and continued throughout the night and the next day. By November 11 the feed supply for the livestock had been exhausted, so McIntosh ordered a detachment to escort the livestock in search of forage.[34] He also allowed an officer and twelve men from each line to hunt for game to feed the soldiers and warned "the men of each party are to keep within sight of each other and report every discovery they make of the Indians."[35] The supply situation improved that afternoon when about seventy men arrived from Fort McIntosh with "a small brigade of pack-horses and some straggling bullocks."[36]

The trek westward resumed at noon the next day. The marchers passed a large spring and saw a tree marked with an Indian war pole and two scalps, assumed to be the scalps of the soldiers killed five days earlier. McIntosh warned the soldiers to be ready for battle and to perform military maneuvers quickly and precisely because "the General is ever anxious for the honour as well as the safety of an army of such brave men... Especially against such enterprising and vigilant enemies as Indians are, who take every advantage and attack with Savage fury."[37]

Snow began falling at sunset on November 13 and continued the next day, forcing the army to remain in camp. A court martial convened and punished two soldiers for firing their guns unnecessarily, "which besides the waste of ammunition where we cannot get supplied is extremely dangerous in our present situation."[38]

"This is the 10th day I have been upon my march" McIntosh reported. "I am not 50 miles from [Fort McIntosh] yet owing to the scandalous pack horses that were imposed upon me." Half of the horses tired from traveling only two or three miles, McIntosh complained, and "the woods is strewed with those that have given out and died. I have now but sixteen miles to Tuscarawas yet I much fear I shall not be able to carry our provisions and stores that length." McIntosh ordered the arrest of two men responsible for supplying the pack horses and provisions.[39]

Messengers from the Delaware tribe came to the American camp and told McIntosh that their warriors would join his army at the Tuscarawas River. McIntosh ordered his soldiers to be "exceeding cautious to distinguish well whether any Indians they meet are friends or enemies before they fire upon them... at the same time every precaution is necessary and to be used against treachery. No man or party of men must be suffered to come in or go out of camp without the General's approbation."[40]

On the afternoon of November 15, the men marched six miles before sunset and set up camp. They marched six miles farther the next day. As they neared the meeting place with the Delaware warriors, McIntosh ordered his soldiers not to conduct personal business with the Indians.[41]

Incessant rainfall kept the army in camp all day November 17. As each passing day depleted the expedition's supplies, the daily ration dwindled to four ounces of half-spoiled flour and eight ounces of poor-quality beef.[42]

The next day McIntosh received intelligence that enemy Indians had been seen near his camp. He cautioned his officers to "Be very careful that none of their men straggle or go outside of their lines by night or day unless they are ordered upon some duty and call their rolls often as the repeated [orders] issued against firing guns wantonly is shamefully neglected... And also that the sentinels have no fires at night. All officers and soldiers are desired to collect and save all the deer's tails they can get and wear them in their hats, which may induce our friend Indians to do the same & distinguish ourselves and them from our enemies."[43]

The army reached its destination on the Muskingum River – formed by the confluence of the Tuscarawas and the Walhonding – on November 18. When the soldiers arrived, they met representatives of their allies among the Delaware tribe. The Delaware "formed themselves with great regularity," a militiaman wrote in his journal, "and when our front advanced near theirs they began the salute with three Indian cheers. From thence a regular fire, which was returned by a hasty running fire round our whole lines, which being done we encamped round our brethren."[44]

On the second day after the army reached the Muskingum, the Indians gave the Americans "a quantity of venison and skins," the militiaman wrote, "and expressed their great grief for the loss of White Eyes their chief but assured the General there was yet many among them that would render him as much service as White Eyes could do was he then alive."[45]

The Delaware asked McIntosh to build a fort at their town "for their defense and safety." McIntosh told them that the fort not only would defend their tribe but also would be part of a path to Detroit. McIntosh appointed the Delaware to spread the word among neighboring tribes that he wanted to meet with them. He would consider any tribes that refused to meet with him to be enemies of the United States and his army would conquer them. Looking around at McIntosh's underfed, ill-equipped troops, the Delaware delegates couldn't help but laugh.[46]

The American soldiers began building what McIntosh envisioned as the second fort on a route to Detroit. He named the new fort after his friend Henry Laurens. The Western Department engineer followed nearly the same four-pointed design for Fort Laurens that he had implemented for Fort McIntosh.[47]

The orderly book entry for November 21 bore bad tidings:

> As the weather begins already to set in very severe and we have experienced the pack horses

to be exceeding sorry, which will make our supplies uncertain, the General is sorry he is obliged to curtail the rations to one pound of flour per man per day until a supply arrives here. And hopes the brave men of his army will content themselves with it for a short time and see the necessity and propriety to make up for the deficiency. Each man is to be served with 1-1/2 lb. of beef per day, which the commissary must strictly observe…

As the General is anxious to have the fort finished and try if we can do anything against the enemy this season, he desires each Regiment to take their share of it in proportion to their number of men… and he hopes they will exert themselves to show who will be done first.[48]

One of the measures McIntosh took to make delivering supplies to the western outposts faster and safer was to build a road from Fort Pitt to Fort McIntosh. The Americans continued to have problems, however, in getting supplies from the east across the mountains to Fort Pitt. Resulting shortages at Fort Pitt caused problems in sending supplies to Fort McIntosh and Fort Laurens. Sending a hundred bushels of salt to Fort Laurens, as McIntosh requested, would leave less than twenty bushels at Fort McIntosh, which would hinder the process of salting beef. "I find that we will be universally distressed for want of salt," a commissary official confided, "that there is not half enough in store here for curing the quantity of beef. …it appears to me that in a few weeks more our beeves in every quarter will be wasted to mere skeletons. I am really very much distressed on the thoughts of this very great misfortune."[49] With beef in short supply, McIntosh allowed daily deer hunts by four men from each regiment at Fort Laurens.[50]

On November 30, McIntosh appointed Captain Abraham Lincoln of the Virginia militia to serve as Deputy Commissary of Hides West of the Mountains and ordered all commissaries, butchers and others who dealt with public hides, leather or shoes to keep Lincoln informed of "their proceedings and the present state of that business."[51] As history continued to unfold, Captain Lincoln would become the grandfather of President Abraham Lincoln.[52]

Fort Laurens remained unfinished when the enlistment periods of the soldiers began to expire. McIntosh refused to leave the job undone, as the entry for December 1 in the orderly book recorded. McIntosh thanked "the spirited officers who engaged the men for a longer time." McIntosh planned to return with the militia from Fort Laurens to Fort McIntosh, where the soldiers would be paid; to keep soldiers from sneaking off early, he directed that no one be paid until they mustered at Fort McIntosh.[53]

The orderly book for December 5 reported the soldiers were "served with a gill of whisky each, and the General is sorry horses could not be procured to bring more of that necessary article. Those who came up with the whiskey are not to have any, as two kegs are missing, to make everyone more careful in the future of what they have in charge."[54]

When construction was completed on December 8, most of the men prepared to return to Fort McIntosh while 150 men garrisoned the new Fort Laurens.[55] As the army returned eastward, some of the militiamen left the main army and traveled in small groups. A Virginia militiamen who experienced his first military service on McIntosh's expedition later recalled that some of the men were so eager to return home that they traveled day and night, "some stopping and making a camp fire, sleep a while, and then push in to Fort McIntosh, not in much order, except each company kept together and all were scattered along, perhaps over half the whole distance."[56]

Provisions remained in short supply, and some of the desperate men ate roasted cowhide. The Virginia militiaman recalled coming across "one poor young fellow named John Bell, sitting by the roadside, crying, saying he was so weak he could not proceed any further." The militiaman shared his meager supply of bread with the young man and "encouraged him to renew the march, which he did, and got in, and finally reached the region of the South Branch of Potomac where he belonged."[57]

A frontiersman escorting supplies from Fort McIntosh to Fort Laurens remembered meeting the army coming the opposite way:

> ...on the head of Yellow Creek, the escort began to meet parties of the militia, rushing on toward the Ohio with all possible speed, the company of militia composing fully one third of the escort joined their companions and

returned, leaving two companies of regulars (of which I was one) to guard the provisions to the fort. Some distance down Sandy Creek, we met General McIntosh, Colonel Brodhead and Colonel Crawford, with the regular troops, and a few militia.[58]

The orderly book indicated that the expedition had returned to Fort McIntosh on December 13:

The General congratulates the troops upon their return to this post on their way home after establishing two important posts in the enemy's country, by which he hopes the safety of the frontiers [will be] secured hereafter, by keeping the savages in awe at home, & preparing the way for further enterprises against them; and the General expects that the most of the gentlemen here will have the honor of finishing in the spring what they have so well began under many difficulties, as the enemy had not the spirit to engage us this time near Tuscaraway as they had promised.

The General returns his hearty thanks to the brave militia of Virginia for a conduct during this campaign which would do honor to the best regular troops, except a few individuals who he hopes will stay at home the next time, & never come here again to poison & corrupt an army so determined to serve their country. That they may not be detained, he desires they may be all mustered this morning… to enable them to make out their pay rolls properly…

As a farther mark of the General's satisfaction with the behavior of the militia he orders them to be served with a pint of whiskey each man, and be discharged immediately after they are mustered, although the time of very few of them is expired yet…[59]

Because the soldiers were weak and emaciated, a ranger from Pennsylvania reported, "the liquor flew to their heads," and nearly two thousand men "were quite inebriated in a few minutes." General McIntosh said "a hair of the same dog was good for the bite, & tomorrow morning you shall all have double rations & another half pint." The ranger noted "none were seen drunk the next day."[60]

The militiamen soon went their various ways. One of the reasons McIntosh had discharged them a short while before their enlistment periods ended was that he did not have enough provisions at Fort McIntosh to continue feeding them. They were not given food for the journey home, so many of them "had to beg supplies, and not unfrequently plunder the fowls of the settlers along the route." A Virginia militiaman reported that he reached his home on the south branch of the Potomac "in good health, on Christmas eve, 1778."[61]

Considering the scarcity of provisions, McIntosh left only one regiment at Fort McIntosh for the winter. McIntosh himself returned to the Western Department headquarters at Fort Pitt.[62]

From Fort Pitt, McIntosh wrote a letter to the vice president of Pennsylvania describing "a good strong fort for the reception and security of prisoners & stores, upon the Indian side of the Ohio below Beaver Creek, with barracks for a regiment; and another upon the Muskingam River, where Colonel Bocquette had one formerly near Tuscarawas, about one hundred miles from this place, which I expect will keep the savages in awe, and secure the peace of the frontiers effectually in this quarter hereafter, if they are well supplied; and will also facilitate any further enterprises that may be attempted that way."[63]

5

Extreme Emergency and Difficulty

Lachlan McIntosh realized that his strategy in the Western Department depended on keeping the forts on the frontier well supplied, which was made difficult by rugged terrain and harsh weather during the winter of 1778-1779.

British officials at Detroit directed attacks against American outposts and settlements on the western frontier. Loyalists and Indian allies sporadically besieged Fort Laurens, the westernmost fort under Lachlan McIntosh's jurisdiction. A party of sixteen men who left the fort to retrieve horses stolen by Indians were lured into an ambush; only one of the men survived.[1]

The 150-man garrison at Fort Laurens faced not only enemy warriors but also severe weather, the threat of starvation, and a debilitating lack of shoes and clothing.

The commander at Fort Laurens reported in December that fourteen soldiers were sick and another fourteen were "Unfit for Duty for Want of Clothing." The report also mentioned that five women were in the fort.[2]

"The distressed situation of the men for clothing prevents the work from going on so briskly as otherwise it would," Colonel John Gibson informed McIntosh, "if any supply of that article should have arrived, please order it forward." Despite the hardship, Gibson told McIntosh, "the men who formerly attempted to mutiny, have behaved extremely well, and unanimity prevails amongst us."[3]

Because "the weather has been very cold and the rivers very high," Gibson wrote, "unless a supply of clothing soon arrives, I shall not have fifty men fit for duty in a short time, which are by no means adequate."[4]

The soldiers gave Fort Laurens the nickname "Fort Nonsense." A letter written by a soldier inside the relative safety of Fort McIntosh on January 29 reports, "Last night there was two Indians come in with an express from fort Nonsense which informed us that Capt. Clark of our regiment and the men that was left there was coming home to join their regiment was attacked on the road within two miles of Tuscarawas & had two killed on the spot and four wounded & one a missing. They fought them till they was reinforced from the fort and then to return with the party back again. There is no account of any of the Indians being killed." The young soldier added, "Give my love to the family & inquiring friends & well-wishers but in particular to the pretty girls."[5]

Referring to the Indian attacks, McIntosh warned an army officer who helped defend the Pennsylvania frontier throughout the Revolution, "I am also informed that a large party of the same people are set off to strike the inhabitants about Ligonier & Black Leg Creek, and send you this express to inform you of it, that you may acquaint the neighborhood and be upon your guard."[6]

McIntosh made plans to send supplies by boat to the desperate men at Fort Laurens. On February 8, 1779, he instructed Major Richard Taylor to transport two hundred kegs of flour from Fort Pitt, fifty barrels of beef and pork from posts at Wheeling and Beaver Creek, "as much whiskey as the Commissary of Issues can spare, some medicines from the Surgeon of the Hospital, and a blacksmith with his tools, and some iron and steel for the use of that garrison, with any other articles, which you know them to stand in need of."[7]

With no way of knowing that supplies were on the way, the commander at Fort Laurens sent a request to McIntosh: "Recommend sending, if not a reinforcement, a supply of provisions and other stores, without delay to this place. You may depend on my defending it to the last extremity, and of my care to prevent surprise. The officers and men here think it is rather hard they should be curtailed in their rations when the troops at the interior posts draw full rations. I am not the least afraid they will forsake me, let what will happen."[8]

McIntosh sent George Washington a report in mid-March on the situation at Fort Laurens:

> … I am sorry to inform you, that contrary to my expectations, things have taken a turn here much for the worse, since I wrote you the 13th of January. The 30th of that month I received an express from Col. Gibson, informing me that one Simon Girty, a renegade among many others found in this place, got a small party of Mingoes, a name by which the Six Nations, or rather Seneca Tribe, is known among the

Western Indians, and waylaid Capt. Clark of the 8th Pennsylvania Regiment with a sergeant and 14 privates, about three miles this side of Fort Laurens, as they were returning after escorting a few supplies from that post, and made Clark retreat to the fort again after killing two and taking one of his men with his saddle bags and all his letters.

Upon hearing this unexpected intelligence, I immediately sent for Cols. Crawford and Brodhead to advise with them upon the best method of supplying that garrison with provisions, of which it was very short, and we had barely horses enough fit for service to transport a sufficient quantity of flour over the mountains for our daily consumption, and scarce of forage for them, altho' they were most worn down. It was, therefore, thought most eligible upon that and other accounts to send a supply by water up Muskingum River by Maj. Taylor, who was charged with that duty.

The 26th of February a scalping party killed and carried off 18 persons, men, women, and children, upon the branches of Turtle Creek, 20 miles east of this, upon the Pennsylvania road, which was the first mischief done in the settlements since I marched for Tuscarawas, and made me apprehensive now that the savages were all inimically inclined, and struck the inhabitants of Westmoreland with such a panic that the great part of them were moving away. While I was endeavoring to rouse the militia, and contriving by their assistance to retaliate, and make an excursion to some Mingo towns upon the branches of Alleghany River who were supposed to have done the mischief, a messenger came to me the 3rd of March instant, who slipt out of Fort Laurens in the night of Sunday the 28th February – by whom Col. Gibson would not venture to write, and informed me that the morning of Tuesday, the 23rd February, a wagoner who was sent out of the fort for the horses to draw wood, and 18 men to guard him, were fired upon, and all killed and scalped in sight of the fort, which the messenger left invested and besieged by a number of Wyandotts, Chippewas, Delawares &c.; and in the last account I had from them, which made me very unhappy, as they were so short of provision, and out of my power to supply them with any quantity, or, if I had it, with men for an escort, since Major Taylor went, who I thought now was inevitably lost; and if I had both, there were no horses to carry it, or forage to feed them, without which they cannot subsist at this season.

In this extreme emergency and difficulty, I earnestly requested the Lieutenants of the several counties on this side of the mountains to collect all of the men, horses, provision and forage they could at any price, and repair to Beaver Creek [Fort McIntosh] on Monday next, the 15th instant, in order to march on that or the next day to Tuscarawas, and if they would not be prevailed on to turn out, I was determined with such of the Continental troops as are able to march, and all the provisions we have, at all events to go to the relief of Fort Laurens, upon the support of which I think the salvation of this part of the country depends.

I have yet no intelligence from the country, that I can depend on. Some say the people will turn out on this occasion with their horses; others, that mischievous persons influenced by our disgusted staff are discouraging them as much as possible. But I am now happily relieved by the arrival of Major Taylor here, who returned with 100 men and 200 kegs of flour. He was six days going up about 20 miles of Muskingum River, the waters were so high and stream so rapid; and as he had above 130 miles more to go, he judged it impossible to relieve Col. Gibson in time, and therefore returned, having lost two of his men sent to flank him upon the shore, who were killed and scalpt by some warriors coming down Muskingum River, and I have my doubts of our only pretended friends, the Delawares of Cooshocking, as none other are settled upon that water.[9]

In an echo of his feuds on the southern frontier, McIntosh's tenure on the western frontier erupted in political rivalries among Virginians and Pennsylvanians along with personal resentment toward McIntosh. His chief critic, Indian agent Colonel George Morgan, referred to "the ignorant, absurd and contradictory conduct and orders of General McIntosh, throughout the whole campaign."[10]

A settler who wanted McIntosh to be replaced by an officer with a record of accomplishment in the Western Department told Congress "we are no nearer now than we was when we first set out" because the command was given to someone "that knew nothing of the matter. The General told me that he was brought up by the sea shore, and that he knew nothing about pack horsing in this wooden [wooded] country." The settler claimed "The General has likewise got the ill will of all his officers, the militia in particular, which I am very sorry for as they are the only people that we have to depend upon to do anything in this Department."[11]

A high-ranking officer under McIntosh's command, Colonel Daniel Brodhead, brought complaints about McIntosh to the attention of Commander in Chief George Washington in January of 1779. "General McIntosh is unfortunate enough to be almost universally hated by every man in this department, both civil & military," Brodhead wrote. "Therefore whatever his capacity may be for conducting another campaign, I fear he will not have it in his power to do anything salutary – I wish my fears may prove groundless but I have no reason to think them so. There is not an officer who does not appear to be exceedingly disgusted, and I am much deceived if they serve under his immediate command another campaign."[12]

Washington waited nearly a month before sending a noncommittal, politically astute reply. Brodhead's complaints "give me that concern which ever arises in my mind from any indication of a want of that harmony and mutual confidence between officers, which the public interest requires," Washington told Brodhead, but "your general assertion and opinion with regard to the dissatisfaction of his officers is by no means a foundation for any measures on my part respecting [McIntosh] that will either convey or imply censure."

Washington added, "The sole reason for appointing General McIntosh to his present command was an opinion of his being in every view qualified for it, and I must observe that while the General was immediately under me, his conduct gave the most favorable impressions of him in every respect."

In conclusion, Washington wrote, "Upon the whole it is my earnest desire that everyone will as far as depends on him – cultivate and promote that good understanding, which is indispensable to the general interest. And I entreat that you will do all in your power to accomplish this desirable end."[13]

Washington confided to a government official that "I wish matters had been more prosperously conducted under the command of General McIntosh." Still, Washington insisted, "during the time of his residence at Valley Forge I had imbibed a good opinion of his good sense – attention to duty, and disposition to correct public abuse, qualifications much to be valued in a separate and distant command."[14]

McIntosh responded to the controversy in the West the same way he responded to the controversy in Georgia, by seeking reassignment. In a resolution dated February 20, 1779, Congress granted McIntosh's request "to retire from" command of the Western Department.[15]

Shortly after Congress granted his request, McIntosh received distressing news from Georgia. A British invasion force had captured Savannah in December of 1778. As a result, McIntosh's wife and younger children living in Savannah had become trapped in enemy territory.

"I am lately informed my own country, all my family, and everything of property I have in the world, are now in the hands of the enemy," McIntosh wrote to his friend Henry Laurens. "I am exceedingly unhappy not to hear anything from them. Desire to be there."[16]

Before he could leave the Western Department, however, McIntosh's sense of duty required him to relieve the beleaguered garrison at Fort Laurens. "I had expected to have set off for Philadelphia before this time," McIntosh told Laurens, "but wishing to leave this Department in as good order as possible, and having some disagreeable intelligence, and unexpectedly, from Fort Laurens, determined me to wait the event."[17]

When he set out to relieve the garrison at Fort Laurens, McIntosh wrote, "all the discontented joined immediately in condemning the executing it, as much as they approved of it before."[18]

While McIntosh urgently prepared to relieve Fort Laurens, the garrison determinedly resisted a siege by British, loyalist and Indian forces. The American soldiers exhausted their provisions during four weeks of siege warfare. For three or four days they subsisted on half a biscuit a day. Then they washed their moccasins, broiled them and ate them. They broiled strips of dried hides. When two men sneaked out of the fort, killed a deer, and brought it back, the soldiers devoured the venison in a few minutes; some of the soldiers chewed raw meat.[19]

Civilian leaders of the territory and the field officers under McIntosh's command all agreed "that Fort Laurens is a post of such consequence, that it should not be evacuated by any means, if it can possibly be kept," McIntosh informed George Washington, "and that it may be defended by 100 men, if provisions cannot be carried for more."[20]

McIntosh personally led a cross-country dash to Fort Laurens. "I am just setting off for Fort Laurens with about two hundred men I have collected of the militia, and better than 300 Continental troops from this garrison and Fort Pitt," he reported to Washington on March 19, "but unfortunately have not collected horses enough to carry the quantity of provision I intended or would be necessary, and as the time will not admit of an hour's delay to wait for any more."[21]

Leaving Colonel Daniel Brodhead at Fort McIntosh to procure more provisions, McIntosh sent Major Richard Taylor to scour the countryside for provisions. McIntosh's department had "not above one month's provisions this side of the mountains," he told Washington. "The difficulty of getting it over, and the distance of carriage, is the grand objection to every enterprise from this quarter."[22]

A local volunteer on the expedition supplied his own "horse, provisions, forage and accoutrements, and instead of being mounted, going out carried a load of flour or bacon on each horse."[23]

Before the relief mission reached Fort Laurens, the siege had been lifted. In a letter to "Brother McIntosh," Captain John Killbuck took credit for persuading the enemy to leave "after much trouble and by frequent speeches to them."[24]

When McIntosh's relief column arrived at Fort Laurens, the famished men inside the fort celebrated noisily, with the consequence of turning their brief sense of salvation into yet another cause for dismay. "A convoy of packhorses arrived, guns fired for joy, horses scared, and run off scattering flour &c," recollected a soldier stationed at Fort Laurens. "This was gathered, and so incautious were many of the men that several made themselves sick with overloading their weak stomachs, and 3 died in consequence."[25]

Most of the next day was spent rounding up the horses that had scattered at the sound of celebratory gunshots.[26]

McIntosh replaced the men who had garrisoned Fort Laurens during the siege with a hundred fresh troops. The rescued soldiers and their rescuers left Fort Laurens two days after the relief column arrived. The return trip proved to be "more tedious than anticipated," a local volunteer remembered, and McIntosh sent an officer "to proceed with all possible speed to Fort McIntosh and return with provision sufficient to subsist the army at least two days; and being piloted by friendly Indians along a path nearer than the main road, we met the army a considerable way back."[27] The forced march from Fort McIntosh to relieve Fort Laurens had taken just over three days, but the return trip took six days because the men and horses were exhausted.[28]

When Lachlan McIntosh returned to Fort Pitt in early April, he learned that George Washington had acted on McIntosh's request to leave the Western Department, and had appointed Colonel Daniel Brodhead to command the department. McIntosh turned over the command on April 5 and left for Philadelphia.[29]

Guarding his sense of honor, as always, McIntosh requested an official investigation of his conduct in the Western Department. "Although I despised the slander I found so industriously spread upon the road as I came down," he told Washington, "I am too tenacious of my own reputation – and the reflection it may occasion upon Your Excellency's judgment in appointing an improper officer to a department – to pass over what may tend to injure either hereafter."[30]

McIntosh supplied a list of more than twenty witnesses on his behalf, including all the officers of the 9th Virginia Regiment, most of the officers of the 8th Pennsylvania Regiment, and Colonel John Gibson, who had commanded the beleaguered garrison at Fort Laurens.[31]

Washington's aide Alexander Hamilton dissuaded McIntosh from insisting on an investigation. "So many principal as well as inferior officers must be called from the Western Department as witnesses that their attendance would entirely disconcert the department," Hamilton wrote to McIntosh. During an investigation, Hamilton pointed out, "You must be detained in a state of military inaction here while you might be usefully serving the public to the Southward."[32]

In his reply, McIntosh agreed with Hamilton's concern that proceedings "might detain me for a considerable time from the more necessary services of my country."[33] He withdrew his application for an investigation.

McIntosh remained anxious about his wife and children who were trapped behind enemy lines in Savannah. Washington gave him an opportunity to go home by assigning him to command the Continental troops in Georgia.

The controversy in the Western Department did not diminish Washington's respect for McIntosh. Washington reported to Congress in May that "General McIntosh's conduct while he acted immediately under my observation was such as to acquire my esteem and confidence; I have had no reason since to alter my good opinion."[34]

Three years of military maneuvering and political infighting in Georgia, Valley Forge, and the Western Department affected McIntosh's appearance so drastically that an acquaintance who passed him on the street in the spring of 1779 did not recognize him.[35]

6

Shrieks from Women and Children

Lachlan McIntosh returned to Georgia in late July of 1779 from his assignments at Valley Forge and the Western Department. He brought with him an infantry regiment and a cavalry squad from Virginia, providing "a seasonal succor and relief to the few militia remaining in the state," a Georgia official observed, "as their own line of the regular army were entirely extinct and annihilated."[1]

Because coastal Georgia lay under British control, McIntosh set up a command post at Augusta. "The few militia in this corner who stick yet to their integrity, and have not joined the enemy, or shamefully left us altogether to ourselves," McIntosh observed, "do not exceed six hundred men."[2] McIntosh asked for help from General Benjamin Lincoln, the commander of the Southern Department, but Lincoln could not spare any troops or supplies.

McIntosh returned to Georgia just in time to participate in an attempt by French and American allies to recapture Savannah. Count d'Estaing sailed to the Georgia coast with a French fleet of thirty-three naval vessels and four thousand troops, including five hundred black soldiers serving as Les Chasseurs-Volontaires de Saint-Domingue. Lincoln led the American army from Charleston toward Savannah.

"I sent an express to General McIntosh who commanded the troops at Augusta," Lincoln wrote in his journal for September 4, "to march with the greatest dispatch with all the men he could collect in 24 hours after he should receive the information, to Ebenezer and to bring down a number of flats, which would facilitate his march as provisions might come in them."[3]

The next day Lincoln urged McIntosh "to the greatest exertions and dispatch as the Count could not remain long on the coast, and that if the infantry could not reach in time he must advance with the horse."[4]

McIntosh apparently concentrated on marching his troops to Savannah quickly, as urged in the second message, instead of sending flatboats downriver to Ebenezer, as requested in the first message.

American cavalry commanded by Count Casimir Pulaski joined McIntosh at Augusta and moved out with him toward Savannah. Reaching the outskirts of Savannah, McIntosh and Pulaski skirmished with pickets in British outposts and established communications with French forces landing at Thunderbolt. McIntosh took a position at Millen's plantation three miles from Savannah and awaited the main American army under Lincoln.[5]

On September 6, Lincoln led the march toward Savannah, leaving William Moultrie in command of the troops defending Charleston. Because McIntosh had not brought down boats from Augusta, Lincoln had to scrounge for vessels to carry his army across the Savannah River. He ordered that a partially completed flat be finished and that a raft be made from boards and timber scavenged from buildings. When troops began crossing the river on the morning of September 12, the raft sank. The army had to cross in a flat that would carry twenty men, a canoe that would carry fifteen, and a larger canoe that would carry thirty. "The troops were mostly thrown across," Lincoln said. He crossed the river in the afternoon and encamped "on the heights of Ebenezer."[6] Lincoln's men spent the next day getting their artillery and wagons across the river and repairing bridges that crossed swampy streams at Ebenezer. Late in the afternoon, McIntosh arrived at Ebenezer with his command.

Moving on from Ebenezer, the American army reached Cherokee Hill, ten miles from Savannah, on September 15. The next day the Americans arrived at Savannah and encamped at Millen's plantation.[7] Lincoln placed McIntosh in command of the 1st and 5th South Carolina Continentals and the Georgia regulars.

On September 16, Count d'Estaing demanded that General Augustine Prevost surrender Savannah to King Louis XVI of France; the count's summons didn't even mention the Americans who were approaching the outskirts of Savannah at that moment. General Prevost answered the summons according to formal European military etiquette, and asked for twenty-four hours to consider the terms of surrender. Count d'Estaing granted the request.

Prevost used the twenty-four hours to finish the fortifications around Savannah and to receive reinforcements who were on their way from Beaufort. Although suffering a fever, Colonel John Maitland evacuated Beaufort on September 12 and sailed across Port

Royal Sound. Convalescents suffering in the southern climate remained on the southwestern side of Hilton Head while eight hundred relatively healthy soldiers transferred from transport vessels to small boats. Because the French fleet blocked the open waterway, Maitland had to find an alternate route to Savannah. Maitland and the first group of his men reached Savannah at noon on September 16 and more men arrived in groups over the next two days.

Once the reinforcements began arriving, Prevost ended the truce on the night of September 17 and defiantly rejected d'Estaing's terms of surrender.

"My God!" American officer Francis Marion exclaimed. "Who ever heard of anything like this before? First allow an enemy to entrench, and then fight him!"[8]

As the twenty-four-hour truce ended, rain began to fall. Siege tactics, such as moving artillery forward, became more difficult on the muddy ground. On September 22, the French Army in three divisions moved into position east of the Ogeechee Road. The Americans encamped to the left of the French in positions reaching to McGillivray's Plantation on the Savannah River. Once the ground began drying, d'Estaing opened siege lines on September 23. The British launched sorties to delay work on the siege approaches.

McIntosh, the second-highest-ranking American officer at Savannah, commanded the right wing of the American army, which included the Georgia militia. An aide to McIntosh, Captain John Lucas, observed "the greatest harmony both of officers and privates while under his command." The militia serving under McIntosh "turned out cheerfully on every occasion, particularly to work in the trenches."[9]

Lachlan McIntosh had returned to Georgia to protect his family, but the fighting at Savannah prevented a reunion. Writing just a few decades after the siege, Georgia's first historian, Hugh McCall, gave this report:

> On the 29th, general M'Intosh solicited general Lincoln's permission to send a flag, with a letter to general Prevost, to obtain leave for Mrs. McIntosh and his family, and such other females and children as might choose to leave the town during the siege, or until the contest should be decided. Major John Jones, aid to general McIntosh, was the bearer of the flag and letter, and found Mrs. McIntosh and family in a cellar, where they had been confined several days. Indeed these damp apartments furnished the only safe retreat, for females and children, during the siege. General Prevost refused to grant the request, imagining that it would restrain the besiegers from throwing bombs and carcasses among the houses to set them on fire.[10]

To hold women and children in harm's way, McIntosh charged, was an act of brutality.[11]

The McIntosh family faced renewed danger when the Americans resumed shelling on October 3. Witnesses reported "great mischief both in town and in the enemy lines."[12] During three days of bombardment, the McIntosh family "suffered beyond description."[13] An account of their ordeal is recorded on a leaf of their family Bible:

> The British officers behaved with great attention and kindness toward Mrs. McIntosh and her children. During the siege, the British provided refuge in the cellar of a house where sick officers were quartered. Mrs. McIntosh nursed the convalescents despite the threat of cannon balls whistling around and perforating the abode. A shell fell into a well near the house and burst, destroying the well and alarming the family, but Mrs. McIntosh was above all fear. Her sons George, Henry and Hampden ran through the streets picking up spent cannon balls; they said they were going to send the ammunition to the Americans.[14]

Major John Jones – the aide to McIntosh who had visited Mrs. McIntosh on September 29 – wrote to his own wife Polly on October 4: "I feel most sincerely for the poor women and children! God only knows what will become of them."[15] On October 7 he wrote Polly, "a more cruel war could never exist than this. The poor women and children have suffered beyond description. A number of them, in Savannah, have already been put to death by our bombs and cannon. …many of them were killed in their beds, and amongst others, a poor woman, with her infant in her arms, was destroyed by a cannon-ball. They have all got into cellars; but even there they do not escape the fury of our bombs, several of them having been mangled in that supposed place of security. I pity General McIntosh; his situation is peculiar. The whole family is there. We have burnt, as yet, only one house; but I expect this night the whole will be in flames."[16]

Jones was slightly inaccurate in saying "the whole family" was trapped in the besieged city. Lachlan and Sarah McIntosh had eight children, but only the five who were younger than twenty stayed with their mother in Savannah: older daughter Esther, who turned eight years old in 1779; younger daughter Catherine; and sons George, Henry Laurens, who was about ten, and John Hampden, who was about nine years old at the time of the siege of Savannah. Their oldest son, Jack, had left Georgia for Jamaica early in the war. Their second son, Lackie, had served in the Western Department with his father and had returned to Augusta by August of 1779.[17] Their third son William, who turned twenty in 1779, served as a captain in the 1st Georgia Continental Battalion and had been taken as a prisoner of war when the British captured Savannah.[18]

The civilian experience during the bombardment was recorded by Anthony Stokes, the colonial Chief Justice of Georgia. In a desperate trip across town, he said, "whenever I came to the opening of a street, I watched the flashes of the mortars and guns, and pushed on until I came under cover of a house; and when I got to the common, and heard the whistling of a shot or shell, I fell on my face. But the stopping under cover of a house was no security, for the shot went through many houses; and Thomson's daughter was killed at the side opposite to that where the shot entered."[19] Adding a grisly detail, Stokes noted that Thomson's daughter "was almost shot in two by a cannon ball."[20]

French artillery, Stokes said, "kept up a brisk cannonade and bombardment; the shot frequently struck near us, and the shells fell on each side of us with so much violence that in their fall they shook the ground, and many of them burst with a great explosion."[21]

Stokes found refuge "at the west end of Yamacraw, which was quite out of the direction of the enemy's batteries. This place was crowded, both inside and out, with a number of whites and negroes, who had fled from the town. Women and children were constantly flocking there, melting into tears, and lamenting their unhappy fate, and the destruction of their houses and property."[22]

As he scurried around Savannah, Stokes observed, "The appearance of the town afforded a melancholy prospect, for there was hardly a house which had not been shot through, and some of them were almost destroyed."[23]

Some of Savannah's civilians sought safety aboard ships on the river, but even there shells plopped into the water around them. Crowds gathered on Hutchinson's Island, where the swampy environment was, Stokes said, "very unwholesome, particularly in the fall."[24] He counted fifty men, women and children huddled in a rice barn on the island.

"Soon almost every family was removed from the town to an island opposite, where they made use of barns," a teenage girl said. "In the barn where I was there were fifty-eight women and children, all intimate friends."[25]

After refusing to let the McIntosh family leave the war zone, General Prevost had a change of heart because his own wife and children also were trapped in Savannah. The Prevost family, along with other women and children, huddled in the basement of a house that had been fortified to make it, as one observer said, "bomb-proof." Workers piled a bank of sand around the house and placed large casks filled with sand along the walls. They also propped up the ceiling of the cellar and covered it with a layer of sand. Feather beds in the basement helped cushion the shock of explosions.[26]

Expressing "sentiments of humanity," Prevost sent a letter to Count d'Estaing: "The houses of Savannah are occupied solely by women and children. Several of them have applied to me that I might request the favour you would allow them to embark on board a ship or ships and go down the river under the protection of yours until this business is decided. If this requisition you are so good as to grant, my wife and children, with a few servants, shall be the first to profit by the indulgence."[27]

Prevost recorded in his journal, "After three hours and a great deal of intermediate cannon and shells, received an insulting answer in refusal from Messrs. Lincoln and d'Estaing conjunctly."[28]

Prevost correctly described the answer from Lincoln and d'Estaing as insulting. "Perhaps your zeal has already interfered with your judgment," they told him. "It is with regret we yield to the austerity of our functions, and we deplore the fate of those persons who will be victims of your conduct, and the delusion which appears to prevail in your mind."[29] Count d'Estaing remained angry over Prevost's previous stalling tactics while awaiting reinforcements. "Such conduct," d'Estaing told Prevost, "is sufficient to forbid every intercourse between us which might occasion the least loss of time."[30] A British officer said Prevost's request was "savagely refused."[31]

While each side blamed the other for endangering women and children, the danger remained. After the allies rejected Prevost's request on October 6, "The cannonade and bombardment continued all night," a man wrote in his journal. The next day the allies directed "most of their fire towards the town, which suffers considerably," he wrote. "At 7 at night the enemy threw several carcasses into the town, and burnt one house." The next day, he wrote, "The Enemy fired little this morning, but during the night cannonaded and bombarded the town furiously."[32]

The allies "opened one of the most tremendous firings I ever heard," a British officer wrote to his wife, "from 37 pieces of cannon – mostly 18-pounders, and 9 mortars, in front, and sixteen pieces of cannon from the river, on our left – mostly 24-pounders. The town was torn to pieces, and nothing but shrieks from women and children to be heard. Many poor creatures were killed in trying to get to their cellars, or hide themselves under the bluff of Savannah River. The firing lasted for some hours."[33]

Although the siege was still in its early stages, d'Estaing became impatient and decided to attack the British troops in their defensive positions. His strategy called on 3,500 French troops in three columns to lead the assault, supported by 1,500 American troops. The allies would make a feint at the British left while making an all-out charge toward the Spring Hill redoubt near the west end of the British line. Count d'Estaing would personally lead the assault, while Lachlan McIntosh would command a second column designated to support the first assault.

The defenders of Savannah included – in addition to British army units – militia from Georgia, South Carolina, North Carolina, and New York. According to one report, the defensive force totaled 7,165 men, including eighty Cherokees and four thousand black men.[34]

The 1st Battalion of the 71st Regiment, a unit that had come through a watery wasteland to reinforce the garrison in Savannah, anchored the east flank. Major Archibald McArthur commanded the battalion because Colonel Maitland, who had led the reinforcements from Beaufort to Savannah, was given a greater responsibility.

Maitland, although mortally ill with a fever, commanded the entire force on the west of the lines. North Carolina loyalists were located on the extreme west flank of the British defenses with the Savannah River at their backs and with Yamacraw Swamp to their right. The 4th Battalion of the 60th Regiment and South Carolina Royalists defended the Spring Hill redoubt on the west side of the lines. The 2nd Battalion of the 71st Regiment took up a position behind the Spring Hill redoubt.[35]

When the French and American allies gathered before dawn on October 9, d'Estaing could tell that the Highland Scots of the 71st Regiment defended the exact place he planned to attack. He could tell by the bagpipes. "At the very moment we came out of the marsh, we were given a serenade which issued from a place quite distant from the one this unit usually occupied," d'Estaing observed. "From it I concluded that the enemy was not only forewarned but also that he wanted to remind us that his best troops were waiting for us. Undoubtedly the soldiers felt inwardly as I did, for the sound of this band appeared to me to have made a profound impression on their morale." He would have called off the attack when he "heard the unexpected sound of these peripatetic bagpipes," d'Estaing wrote, "had we not been so far advanced and had not had the Americans for companions, or rather, for masters."[36]

Firing began when the sun rose. French troops swarmed out of the morning mist across open ground toward the British defenses. French grenadiers cut through the abatis with hatchets and broke the British line.

The British troops stubbornly defended their position on the Spring Hill redoubt. General Prevost reported that an officer on the redoubt "nobly fell with his sword in the body of the third he had killed with his own hand."[37]

Faced with such fierce resistance, the French retreated. Count d'Estaing rallied his men to charge once again. They became trapped in the entrenchments near Spring Hill redoubt and were cut to pieces by musket balls and grape shot. In the frantic fighting, d'Estaing himself was wounded several times.

John Laurens' light infantry and Francis Marion's 2nd South Carolina Regiment resumed the attack on the redoubt. Under heavy fire, Marion led his regiment across the moat and into the abatis. Sergeant William Jasper, who had distinguished himself in 1776 by rescuing the flag at Fort Sullivan, suffered a mortal wound while trying to rescue the regimental colors at the Spring Hill redoubt.

As the Americans of the 2nd Regiment carried their colors, a French soldier took the fleur-de-lis of France to the walls of the Spring Hill redoubt. The allies could not scale the parapet under fire, and were ordered to retreat. Despite his wounds, d'Estaing ordered a drummer to signal the French troops to gather around him for yet another assault.

To repel the repeated allied assaults, the British called in reserves. "At this most critical moment," General Prevost wrote, "Major Glasier of the 60th Grenadiers and the marines, advancing rapidly from the lines, charged, it may be said, with a degree of fury. In an instant the ditches of the redoubt and a battery to its right in rear were cleared, the grenadiers charging head long into them, and the enemy drove in confusion over the abatis and into the swamp."[38]

Casimir Pulaski led two hundred cavalrymen on a dash between the British defensive works. Canister shot pierced Pulaski's chest and thigh.[39]

At this point Lachlan McIntosh led the American reserve column to the foot of the Spring Hill redoubt. McIntosh surveyed a scene of confusion and desperation.

His friend John Laurens asked if McIntosh knew where half of Laurens' troops had gone.

When McIntosh approached d'Estaing for orders, Major Thomas Pinckney served as their translator. "Inform him that my column is fresh," McIntosh told Pinckney. "Ask him to direct me where, under present circumstances, I should make the attack."[40] The count ordered McIntosh to move to the left and stay out of the way of the French troops. To follow d'Estaing's orders, McIntosh had to lead his column through the wet, boggy Yamacraw Marsh. A British vessel in the Savannah River opened fire on McIntosh's column. By the time McIntosh crossed the marsh, the sound of battle had faded. McIntosh sent Pinckney to high ground to reconnoiter. Pinckney reported that the allies had retreated. McIntosh then led his column, still under heavy grape-shot fire, away from the battleground.[41]

Estimates of British casualties range from sixteen to forty killed and thirty-nine to sixty-three wounded.

On the allied side, the French reported 151 men killed and 370 wounded while the Americans combined reports of killed and wounded for a total of 231 casualties. Two hundred bodies were buried around the Spring Hill redoubt.[42]

Among the American dead was Major John Jones, the aide to McIntosh who had visited the McIntosh family behind enemy lines. Before the battle he had experienced a premonition of death and bade his comrades a fond farewell.[43] Jones had written his last letter to his wife Polly four days before the battle and she received it at her refuge in South Carolina after his death. "Adieu, my good wife," he had written, "and believe me to be, with sincerity, your ever affectionate, John Jones."[44]

Count d'Estaing raised the siege on October 18 and evacuated the French forces by sea. General Lincoln led the main American army back across the Savannah River on October 19 and returned to Charleston.

McIntosh, still worried about his family in Savannah, made preparations to withdraw the troops under his command. Many of his soldiers, however, disappeared into the countryside. Many others were sick or wounded. He had trouble finding enough able-bodied men to serve as guards. Leaving his family behind enemy lines in the war-ravaged city, he led the remnant of his force away from Savannah.

In late December, McIntosh learned that the British were willing to allow his wife and children to leave Savannah. At this point he put his family responsibilities ahead of his military duties, and he turned to a family member – his older brother – for help. Accompanied only by his brother William and a few servants, Lachlan hurried from Augusta to make the arrangements to free his wife and children. Bitter winter weather slowed their progress.

As the coldest night of the year descended, the traveling party stopped at a hut beside the road. The men went inside to build a fire before unpacking the gear on their horses. Bandits stormed into the hut. One bandit pointed his gun at Lachlan McIntosh and pulled the trigger, but the gun misfired. Lachlan wrested the gun away.

Lachlan then struck another gunman and deflected a shot overhead. Lachlan, William, and their servants fought their way clear of the bandits and escaped out the back door of the hut. The bandits plundered the baggage on the horses, taking not only supplies but also personal belongings and papers.[45] Lachlan's ongoing struggle to free his family from enemy territory once again encountered frustration.

Not long after William and Lachlan McIntosh fended off roadside bandits, they learned that their younger brother George had died. Lachlan had been especially close to George since the two of them had gone to Charleston when they were young. Political accusations against George had led to the duel between Lachlan and Button Gwinnett, which forever changed Lachlan's military career. George had been in poor health when Gwinnett caused George to be thrown in the common jail. His health worsened during the tribulations that followed, including the looting of his plantation by men associated with Gwinnett. Shortly before he set out on horseback from Georgia to Philadelphia to state his case before Congress, George described himself as "a mere skeleton, worn off his legs and hardly able to stand."[46] George was just forty years old when he died in December of 1779. Sir Patrick Houstoun and George Houstoun, brothers of George's late wife, became guardians of George's seven-year-old son John Houstoun McIntosh. Patrick and George Houstoun also were appointed as administrators of George's estate along with Robert Baillie, the husband of George's sister Ann. George owned thirteen thousand acres in South Georgia and a lot in Savannah. His slaves were appraised at £3,762. Because his home had been looted in 1777, he had only seventeen pieces of silver such as spoons and old plate.[47]

When Lachlan got the grim news of his younger brother's death, he set out from Augusta for George's plantation Rice Hope near Darien. Arriving several days after the funeral, Lachlan looked through George's papers and saved the grants and titles to George's land at the headwaters of the Sapelo River. Lachlan engaged a wagoner to carry a parcel of indigo from the plantation to Charleston, where it would be safe from the British forces occupying coastal Georgia. George's personal belongings were left in the care of the plantation overseer as Lachlan hurried to leave his family homeland that had become enemy territory.[48]

7

The Last Extremity

Lachlan McIntosh strove in vain to keep his family safe during the American Revolution. When border warfare engulfed the family home at Darien, Lachlan moved his wife Sarah and their five youngest children to the relative safety of Savannah. Then the British captured Savannah, trapping Sarah and the children behind enemy lines. By early January of 1780 when Sarah and the children were "thrown over to Carolina with only the bare clothes they had on," as Lachlan put it, coastal South Carolina had become a war zone.[1]

A hundred ships carrying 8,708 British troops had sailed from New York to threaten Charleston. In early February, British troops took position just south of Charleston, and a British fleet blockaded Charleston Harbor.

Lachlan decided to take Sarah and the children to the backcountry of South Carolina, and obtained leave from General Lincoln "to fix my family." Lachlan and his family set out with two wagons on February 13 and crossed the Edisto River at Parker's Ferry. The next day they crossed the headwaters of the Ashley River at Dorchester and proceeded to Goose Creek, where they "were detained this night and all the next day & night," according to Lachlan's journal.[2]

The McIntosh family joined a stream of refugees fleeing the coast for the backcountry. On February 16, they met Continental General Isaac Huger "with his family at Monks Corner going up the country," Lachlan wrote. Learning that the ferry at Moncks Corner was "impassable with carriages," Lachlan took his family farther up the Congaree River to Nelson's Ferry. On February 18, the McIntosh family crossed the Congaree "with much difficulty" and found lodging at Colonel Thomas Sumter's home, "where we were weather bound all the next day and night and very genteelly treated."[3]

When the wintry weather relented, Lachlan tried to find a home away from home for his family in the healthful environment of the High Hills of Santee, but other refugees had already filled all of the houses in the neighborhood. The family moved on, spending a night in "a little inhospitable house," before arriving at the outskirts of Camden, the principal town of the South Carolina backcountry.[4]

At Camden the McIntosh family was greeted by old friends, including fellow refugees from Georgia and "my old friend & acquaintance" Joseph Kershaw of Camden. "Moved this evening to a little shop in Camden, which was the only vacant house Colo. Kershaw could procure for me," Lachlan wrote on February 29. General Huger had already reserved the shop, however, and the McIntosh family would have to leave if the Huger family came to Camden. Kershaw "was kind enough to promise he would supply my family with provision during my absence,"

Lachlan wrote, "& took the few slaves I had left to work with his own, upon shares."[5]

Lachlan stayed in Camden about a week while making arrangements for the well-being of his family. He had spent only two months with Sarah and the children since they had been released from Savannah. Before that, his assignments at Valley Forge and the Western Department, together with their captivity in Savannah, had separated him from them for more than two years. Now the war would separate them again. On March 8, Lachlan began the return trip to Charleston. The next day he crossed paths with his son Lackie, who was traveling from Charleston toward Camden to check on the family.[6]

Lachlan heard cannon fire on March 11 as he approached Charleston, the city where he had lived as a young man. After he reported for duty at General Lincoln's quarters, he and Lincoln looked out from a house on Tradd Street and observed British troop transports, supply ships, merchant vessels, and war ships preparing to support a siege. The British had already erected an artillery battery on James Island across the harbor from Charleston and within a few days would mount heavy artillery on the south bank of the Ashley River near the city.[7]

McIntosh had arrived in Charleston as a brigadier general without a brigade. Lincoln ordered McIntosh to command eleven militia units from North Carolina and South Carolina lumped together as a "Brigade of Coventry" with a total of about twelve hundred men.

Lincoln posted the militia in batteries along the waterfront.[8]

McIntosh noted in his journal entry for March 17 that "my family, servants, horses, &ca. were moved yesterday to new quarters, Mr. Lowndes' house where General Hogan lodged, near Ferguson's."[9]

At Charleston, McIntosh once again served with the Chevalier de Cambray-Digny, an engineer who had laid out McIntosh's new forts in the Western Department in 1778 and designed the defenses of Charleston in 1780.[10] During their stint in the Western Department, McIntosh had described Cambray as "a gentleman of real merit."[11]

McIntosh also reunited with Colonel Thomas Clark, who had served under McIntosh's command at Valley Forge and had assumed command of the North Carolina Brigade when McIntosh was appointed to the Western Department. Since then, Clark had been deployed to the South and had been wounded at Stono Ferry in June of 1779 before participating in the defense of Charleston.[12]

McIntosh had been in Charleston less than a week when political rivalries in Georgia once again disrupted his career. Georgia Governor George Walton had delivered to the Continental Congress a document approved by the Georgia Assembly, according to Walton, that said "It is to be wished we could advise Congress that the return of Brigadier General McIntosh gave satisfaction to either the militia or Confederals: but the common dissatisfaction is such, and that grounded on weighty reasons, it is highly necessary that Congress would, whilst that officer is in the service of the United States, direct some distant field for the exercise of his abilities."[13]

In a closely split vote, Congress resolved that "a copy of the letters from the State of Georgia, as far as they related to General McIntosh, be transmitted to that officer, and that he be informed Congress deem it inexpedient to employ him at present in the southern army, and therefore, that his services in that department be dispensed with, until the further order of Congress."[14]

The president of Congress wrote a letter on February 15 informing McIntosh of his suspension, and McIntosh received the letter on March 17.[15]

Throughout his career, McIntosh went into a rage whenever his honor was at stake, and this dishonor was especially hard to bear. His anger was evident when he showed the letter to General Lincoln and to South Carolina Governor John Rutledge, the highest authority over the South Carolina militia. After examining the letter and studying the political accusations that instigated it, they told him to remain at his post as long as the garrison was under siege.[16]

Since McIntosh commanded militia rather than Continental troops, Lincoln and Rutledge were not, in a strictly literal interpretation, defying the decision of Congress.

McIntosh contacted William Glascock, the speaker of the Assembly in Georgia who purportedly had signed the letter to Congress. Glascock responded that the letter was a forgery and that he detested "the ungenerous and unjust attack" on McIntosh's reputation."[17]

Glascock also informed Congress that the letter was "a flagrant forgery, of which I disclaim all knowledge whatever." He added, "I am glad of the opportunity of informing Congress that so far is that forgery from the truth that I believe there is not a reputable citizen or officer of Georgia but who would be happy in serving under General McIntosh." Glascock said that McIntosh "ought to receive the grateful testimonials of public approbation instead of the malicious insinuations of private slander, in which class I am under the necessity of ranking the forged letter." The slanderous insinuations, Glascock said, showed "extreme malice and rancor of General McIntosh's enemies" who are "governed by design or self-interest."[18]

The military situation in Charleston deteriorated when British warships crossed the bar into the harbor on March 20. On March 29, British troops crossed the Ashley River onto the Charleston Peninsula. The troops then moved into position to lay siege to the town.

The Americans sent a light infantry brigade commanded by Lieutenant Colonel John Laurens to impede the British advance. The brigade took position in a small fortification a mile outside of town. About a mile farther out of town, a detachment of riflemen hid in the woods alongside the road. When the British arrived at noon on March 30, the riflemen ambushed the lead column. The opening volley wounded Lord Caithness, an aide to General Clinton. The British counterattacked, driving the American riflemen down the road toward Charleston. A running battle continued for half an hour.

When the riflemen returned to their brigade, Laurens and Major Edward Hyrne rode out of the fortification to reconnoiter. Hessian troops fired from a hidden position in the trees. Hyrne was wounded and fell from his horse. Laurens drove off the riderless horse to keep the British from taking it, and helped Hyrne back into the fortification. Lincoln sent orders to Laurens to abandon the position. The opposing troops exchanged fire as the Americans withdrew. Hessians occupied the fortification.

Late in the afternoon, Laurens ordered a counterattack. A bayonet charge drove the Hessians out of the fortification. After the attack, Laurens found a dead Hessian holding Hyrne's hat.

British light infantry drove the American brigade back out of the fortification. Skirmishing continued until evening. When darkness fell, Laurens' brigade was inside the American lines at Charleston.[19]

On April 2, the British broke ground on their siege works in front of Charleston. The besiegers and defenders began bombarding one another with cannon and mortars.

After dark on April 5, the British battery on Fenwick's Point and the galleys in Wappoo Cut opened fire on the town, damaging several houses. Observers in the British lines heard Charlestonians screaming and wailing.

The next night the cannonade continued, killing a carpenter and doing mayhem. The bombardment hit close to home for Lachlan McIntosh: two cannonballs went through McIntosh's quarters, five balls struck Mr. Ferguson's house and outbuildings in front of McIntosh's quarters, and the shelling killed two of McIntosh's horses in the yard.[20]

The British commanders issued a summons on April 10. They gave the Americans a chance to surrender, offering the alternatives "of saving their lives and property contained in the town, or of abiding by the fatal consequences of a cannonade and storm."[21]

Lincoln, perhaps because the people of Charleston had vilified him for placing their homes and property at risk in his campaigns of the previous year, notified Clinton he would not surrender. He still had the option of evacuating the American army by boat up the Cooper River toward Moncks Corner.

"Between nine & ten this morning the Enemy opened all their gun & mortar batteries at once (being the first time they fired upon the Town or our lines upon the front)" McIntosh noted in his journal entry for April 13, "& continued a furious cannonade & bombarding with little intermissions till midnight." The artillery killed a sergeant and a private from North Carolina, "& some women & children in Town." Because of the barrage "the Houses are much damaged and two were burned down" and an American artillery battery was damaged.[22]

Facing the possibility that Charleston might fall to British forces, Governor Rutledge and part of the state council left on April 13 to avoid capture and provide for ongoing civil government in South Carolina. Lincoln convened the general officers to consider evacuating the American army. McIntosh wrote in his journal that "without hesitation I gave it as my own opinion that as we were so unfortunate as to suffer ourselves to be penned up in the Town, & cut off from all resources in such circumstances, we should not lose an hour longer in attempting to get the Continental Troops at least out, while we had one side open yet over Cooper River."

McIntosh observed that "the salvation not only of this State but some other" depended on preserving the Continental troops of the Southern Department; his reference to "some other" state apparently reflected his concern for his home state of Georgia.

Lincoln said he needed time to make a decision and would convene another meeting for further discussion.[23]

"The Enemy are approaching fast upon the right," McIntosh wrote the next day, "& keep up an incessant fire from their small arms, cannon, and mortars." The shelling killed a sergeant from North Carolina, and three men were killed "by two of our cannon going off while they were loading them."[24]

Artillery fire from James Island struck a church steeple and damaged a statue of English political leader William Pitt that stood in downtown Charleston. The barrage killed a Charleston resident and wounded a woman who was in bed with him. A cannon ball killed an aide to General William Moultrie, small arms fire killed two men, and artillery shells wounded three men. "Also two French men wounded," McIntosh reported, "one lost a leg & the other an arm." A soldier on sentry duty "had an arm shot off by our own cannon," McIntosh reported, and "a twelve pounder burst in the Horn Work by which two men were much hurt." As the British worked closer to the American lines, McIntosh observed, "the Enemy do not now throw large shells as they have done, but showers of small ones from their mortars and howitzers, which prove very mischievous, especially on our right where one man was killed & two wounded of the North Carolinians."[25]

While most of the British forces manned siege lines just outside of Charleston, other British forces crossed the Cooper River and defeated Americans stationed at Moncks Corner on April 14. The loss of Moncks Corner was disastrous to American forces in Charleston, because it endangered their route of escape across the Cooper River and also cut off food and other supplies coming from the backcountry.

When General Lincoln called a council of American officers on April 19, some of them continued to advocate evacuating the army. Previously, McIntosh and William Moultrie had prepared a written plan for evacuating the army, but McIntosh noted "the difficulty appeared much greater now." Responding to the new situation, "I proposed leaving the Militia for the guards &ca. in garrison until the Continental Troops cleared themselves." When McIntosh proposed evacuating the Continental Army and leaving the militia to guard Charleston, he was offering to sacrifice his personal welfare for the good of the army. Since he had been placed in command of militia when he arrived in

Charleston and since he had been suspended from service as a Continental officer, he presumably would have remained with the militia when the Continental troops retreated across the Cooper River.[26]

McIntosh's proposal was argued down by other officers, who wanted to ask the British for honorable terms of surrender. At that point, Lieutenant Governor Christopher Gadsden arrived. Gadsden, who was the highest-ranking civilian official in Charleston after Governor Rutledge left, "appeared surprised & displeased that we had entertained a thought of capitulation or evacuating the garrison."[27] If the military officers did decide to surrender, Gadsden said, he would consult the civilian council and provide articles of capitulation that would be required by the citizens of Charleston.

Later that evening the officers agreed to seek honorable terms of surrender. Gadsden and four civilian leaders stormed into the meeting and spoke "very rudely," McIntosh wrote, "the Lieutenant Governor declaring he would protest against our proceedings." Implying that members of the South Carolina militia were more determined than the Continental troops, Gadsden said "the Militia were willing to live upon rice alone rather than give up the town upon any terms." Gadsden claimed that "even the old women were so accustomed to the Enemy's shot now that they traveled the streets without fear or dread." Gadsden, however, deferred to the military officers and told them "if we were determined to capitulate that he had his terms in his pocket ready."[28]

Another civilian official, Thomas Ferguson, showed hostility toward the military officers. The residents of Charleston, he said, "would keep a good watch upon us the army" and if the troops boarded boats to evacuate across the Cooper River "he would be among the first who would open the gates for the Enemy and assist them in attacking us before we got aboard."[29]

After Gadsden's party left, Colonel Charles Cotesworth Pinckney "came in abruptly upon the council, & forgetting his usual politeness, addressed General Lincoln in great warmth & much the same strain as the Lt. Governor had done, adding that those who were for business required no councils & that he came over on purpose from Fort Moultrie to prevent any terms being offered the Enemy or evacuating the garrison."[30]

The rude Charlestonians offended McIntosh's tender sense of honor. He felt "so much hurt by the repeated insults given to the Commanding Officer in so public a manner, & obliquely to us all through him, that I could not help declaring as it was thought impracticable to get the Continental Troops out I was for holding the garrison to the last extremity." They had, he declared, "already come to the last extremity." If anyone felt that the last extremity had not arrived, he "desired to know what we called the last extremity."[31]

The meeting ended with the military officers giving sway to the civilian leaders and agreeing to continue holding out against the siege. The next day the officers met again and agreed that they could not hold out much longer and that evacuation would be almost impossible now that

British troops had taken positions on the opposite side of the Cooper River. The Americans tried to negotiate an end to the siege under "honorable terms of capitulation." They wanted their army to be allowed to withdraw from town and live to fight another day. They also wanted security for the residents of Charleston and their property. The British rejected the terms. That night, British artillery bombarded Charleston "with greater virulence & fury than ever, & continued it without intermission till daylight," McIntosh observed. "The killed & wounded lately are so many they cannot be ascertained."[32]

The besiegers continued their relentless approach while the besieged grew more desperate. "Our ration this day ordered to be reduced to ¾ lb. of beef," McIntosh recorded in his journal on April 22. "The Enemy kept up a heavy cannonade, & approach fast on our left in front of the advanced redoubt or Half Moon battery – three men wounded &ca."[33]

The Americans continued to fight back. At daylight on April 24 two hundred Virginians and South Carolinians launched a surprise sortie. Using bayonets, the Americans killed fifty British soldiers inside the siege trenches and took twelve prisoners. Two American privates were wounded and Captain Thomas Moultrie, a brother of General William Moultrie, was killed in the sortie.

That night a rifle ball killed a colonel from Virginia when he looked over the parapet of the Half Moon battery. "Two privates killed also & seven wounded, with several others not known," McIntosh wrote, "having kept an incessant fire of cannon, mortars & small arms on both sides."[34]

As British forces advanced downstream on the opposite bank of the Cooper River from Charleston, American units withdrew from that side of the river. A North Carolina regiment of about two hundred soldiers left Lempriere's Point and joined forces with McIntosh's brigade in Charleston.[35] John Laurens also evacuated his light infantry from Lempriere's Point and resumed his defense of the Horn Work in Charleston. The British occupied Lempriere's Point and Haddrell's Point on April 25 and captured Fort Moultrie on May 7. Until then, the Americans had controlled the crossing of the Cooper between Lampriere's Point and Charleston, and had been able to bring beef and other provisions into the besieged city; once the Americans abandoned the opposite side of the Cooper River they faced eventual starvation.

Like the Americans in Charleston, British besiegers endured roaring artillery exchanges, debilitating heat, irritating mosquitoes and enervating sleeplessness. Inevitably, the fog of war befell the besiegers. On April 25 one group of British soldiers mistook another group of British soldiers for American attackers and opened fire on their own comrades. In the melee, seven British soldiers were killed and twenty-one were wounded. McIntosh was on duty at the time and listened in the dark as British soldiers "gave several huzzas, & abused us, calling us bloody dogs."[36]

As the siege neared culmination, McIntosh described the inexorable deterioration of the American defenses. "Tar barrels ordered to be fixed before our lines every evening & burn all night to prevent a surprise, as the Enemy are close to the canal, & keep up almost a continued running fire of small arms night & day upon us," he wrote on April 27. "A picket of a field officer & 100 men of my Militia Brigade ordered every evening to Gadsden's old house, to support a small guard of a sergeant & 12 regulars upon the wharf in case of an attack by the Enemy boats upon that quarter."[37]

With the British siege lines so near the American defensive works, the Americans anticipated an assault. "General Lincoln informed the General Officers privately that he intended the Horn Work as place of retreat for the whole army in case they were drove from the Lines," McIntosh wrote on April 29. "I observed to him the impossibility of those who were stationed at the South Bay & Ashley River retreating there in such case, to which he replied that we might secure ourselves as best we could. A heavy bombardment from the Enemy during the night & small arms never ceasing. A Deserter from them says they are preparing a bridge to throw over the canal. Capt. Templeton of the 4th Georgia Regiment wounded by a shell."

The next day McIntosh reported that "severe firing of cannon, mortars & small arms continued on both sides. Lt. Campen & Ensign Hall of North Carolina wounded badly, & Lt. Philips of the Virginians. The number of privates killed and wounded not known because there are so many."[38]

General Lincoln called the American generals together to discuss their next move. During the meeting, an officer who had recently arrived from Philadelphia presented the printed resolution of Congress suspending McIntosh from command in the Southern Department of the Continental Army. McIntosh reported that the resolution "was laid before Council" but does not report what response, if any, the generals made. McIntosh continued to serve as a commander of militia as assigned by Lincoln seven weeks earlier.[39]

On May 4, McIntosh recorded, rations were reduced to six ounces of poor-quality meat, rice and coffee with sugar.[40] McIntosh did not continue his journal of the siege after his entry for May 4. At about that time, the British overran the batteries where McIntosh's militia brigade was posted, and he was taken as a prisoner of war.[41]

8

Calamities of War

The American army in Charleston surrendered to British besiegers on May 12, 1780. The British took possession of the town, fortifications, artillery, public stores, and shipping at the wharves.

British officers listed their casualties during the Siege of Charleston as seventy-eight killed and 189 wounded. On the American side, eighty-nine American soldiers and twenty civilians were killed during the siege and 138 American soldiers were wounded.[1]

Most of the five hundred militiamen who surrendered were given their parole within a week of the surrender and began walking home. The residents of Charleston also were considered prisoners on parole.

Close to four thousand Continental troops were taken as prisoners of war. Continental enlisted men and non-commissioned officers were housed in barracks near the edge of town. Hundreds of them escaped individually or in groups as large as thirty. In August, the British transferred the captives to prison ships in the harbor, where nearly four hundred sickened and died in unsanitary, crowded conditions. By the time prisoners were exchanged more than a year later, the number of enlisted men had been cut in half.[2]

After the surrender ceremony, Lachlan McIntosh and the other Continental officers returned to their quarters in Charleston for a few days while they collected their baggage and signed their paroles. Under the terms of capitulation, the officers were allowed to keep their swords, pistols and baggage and to retain their servants.[3]

On the morning of May 18, the officers were transported across Charleston Harbor to Haddrell's Point. When they arrived, General William Moultrie reported, "it was very difficult to get quarters in barracks, for the number of officers that were sent over; they went to the neighboring houses, within the limits of their paroles; and many of them built huts about in the woods, and in a little time were comfortably settled with little gardens about them; the number of officers (prisoners) at Haddrell's Point and the adjacent houses were two hundred and seventy-four."[4] Moultrie added that he and Colonel Charles Pinckney resided in "excellent quarters" on the Pinckney estate called Snee Farm five miles from Haddrell's Point.[5]

Logistical problems snarled the supply system for the prisoners. Ten days after the prisoners arrived, Moultrie complained "that our provisions are very irregularly served out to us; sometimes three days' bread and two days' meat; at other times, half day's rations of beef and full rations of flour; in short we have been almost starved; crabs and fish have supported us hereto."[6] A month later Moultrie once again reported the prisoners at Haddrell's Point were "irregularly served with provisions" due to difficulties in finding a suitable boat in time to catch a favorable tide for crossing the harbor. The only boat available, Moultrie said, "is used with great risk, both to the men and provisions, as one hand is employed almost constantly to bale."[7] Moultrie asked British authorities to provide a large canoe to supply provisions weekly.

McIntosh wrote to his wife Sarah "we must confess we have hitherto had a sufficient allowance of good salt provision but cannot boast of any luxury unless it is a little fish we catch at times ourselves, which serves also for amusement and a necessary exercise."[8] The officers remained in the Haddrell's Point vicinity while arrangements were made to exchange them for British officers. "The limit of the general officers is the little parish of Christ Church opposite to Charleston, which we cannot complain of," McIntosh informed his wife.[9]

During the summer some of the officers and servants at Haddrell's Point suffered from yellow fever and requested medicine from the British hospital. "I have kept my health pretty well since I have been a prisoner," Lachlan assured Sarah.[10]

Morale plummeted among the officers enduring prolonged confinement as prisoners of war. Moultrie observed that the officers became "ungovernable indeed, and it was not much to be wondered at, when two hundred and fifty of them from different states were huddled up together in the barracks, many of them of different dispositions, and some of them very uncouth gentlemen; it is not surprising that there should be continual disputes among them and frequent duels. General McIntosh, who was the senior officer that resided constantly with them, complained to me of their disorderly conduct and uncivil behavior to each other."[11]

Moultrie threatened to punish officers who violated military discipline. He asked McIntosh to "let them know that I think myself fully authorized for that purpose, notwithstanding that we are prisoners of war, and should any disorders happen, you will apply to me, and I will immediately order a court martial to be held."[12]

The officers found an excuse to relieve the drudgery of imprisonment when July 4 arrived. They celebrated the anniversary of the signing of the Declaration of Independence with a dinner and "decent festivity,"[13] according to Moultrie. Later in the evening, after Moultrie had left, prisoners illuminated some of the windows of the barracks and fired pistols and fowling pieces. The commander of a nearby British fort complained "the conduct of the rebels" was "very irregular and improper. Not contented to celebrate this day of their supposed Independence with music, illuminations, etc., they have presumed to discharge a number of small arms, which, I imagine, it is thought that they were not (nor indeed ought not to be, by the articles of capitulation) to be in possession of."[14] The British commandant in Charleston demanded that the prisoners give up all their firearms. Moultrie replied that the articles of capitulation stipulated that the officers could keep their pistols and that a letter from Sir Henry Clinton "permitted the officers to amuse themselves with their fuzees."[15] In the end, the officers were allowed to keep their pistols but Moultrie instructed McIntosh to collect the fowling pieces and turn them over to British authorities.[16]

Months of captivity rolled by, and Moultrie reported in late December that the barracks at Haddrell's Point were "so unfinished as to make them very cold and disagreeable in a winter season."[17] By March of 1781, additional Continental officers taken prisoner in ongoing warfare had been sent to Haddrell's Point, making conditions "exceedingly crowded."[18]

Lachlan McIntosh and several other officers were paroled in the summer of 1781 and traveled from Charleston to Philadelphia under a flag of truce.[19]

Robert Baillie, the husband of Lachlan's sister Ann, tried to help his in-laws while McIntosh was imprisoned. A former British officer in colonial Georgia, Baillie was "a professed Tory, or advocate for the old British government, but deemed a very honest man," reported a pamphlet published in 1777. When discussing American independence, the McIntosh brothers and Baillie "always differed so much that they were (though otherwise on good terms) ever contesting and wrangling on their political sentiments when and wherever they met."[20]

After the British captured Savannah and Charleston, Baillie's loyalist sentiments put him in a position of influence. He informed his imprisoned brother-in-law that he had worked with British officials "to procure you the liberty of coming to live with us till you should be exchanged."[21] Learning that McIntosh had gone to

Philadelphia, Baillie congratulated him on getting out of the prisoner of war barracks but "at the same time I must confess I should have been much better pleased to have seen you here and entirely detached from the American interests; however, I know your sentiments and will therefore say no more upon that subject."[22] Baillie added, "Poor Nancy has been flattering herself with the hopes of seeing you but will now be greatly disappointed."[23]

Knowing his brother-in-law would want news of their family, Baillie wrote "Your sister and the children are very well and Little John who is now with us and very hearty." Baillie reported seeing Lachlan's older brother William and his family a few days before writing the letter. William, who considered himself a prisoner on parole, had taken up residence on the St. John's River in British East Florida near the Georgia border. Because an exchange of prisoners of war was underway, Baillie reported, William would have to choose between leaving Florida or becoming a British subject; "he seems determined to prefer the former and I suppose must soon go to the northward."[24]

Baillie told Lachlan "I beg to hear from you, and if you will give me any directions respecting your Georgia affairs you may depend upon my doing the best I can for your interests."[25] Referring to Lachlan's son Jack, who had left Georgia at the beginning of the war, Baillie said "I have not heard from Jamaica this great while; I expected to have seen your son here before this but have been disappointed. I am convinced his presence would have been to some service in your affairs."[26] The raids and counter-raids of border warfare together with civil seizures by patriot and

British governments had destroyed the wealth of the extended family. William's financial situation was "really much distressed," Baillie wrote. "My own situation is indeed very little better for though I am not yet sued, the debts I owe, with interest accumulating for these five years past, amounts to a sum I shall never be able to pay and my property is so greatly reduced that I can hardly support my family in any decent manner."[27]

Baillie summed up the situation they faced together. "This cursed war has ruined us all. However, I still flatter myself it will soon be at an end, and that we shall again be able to return to our plantations and live peaceably together, which I assure I most sincerely wish for."[28]

While Lachlan McIntosh languished as a prisoner of war, his family stayed on the move in search of refuge. Lachlan had escorted his wife Sarah and younger children to Camden before reporting to duty at Charleston. Soon after the British took control of Charleston, however, Camden became the center of British operations in the backcountry. Sarah had already endured life behind British lines during the Siege of Savannah, which may be why she decided to leave Camden. The McIntosh family may have left Camden at the same time when Colonel Buford withdrew and Governor Rutledge escaped. Sarah, who was forty-one years old in 1781, relied on her twenty-three-year-old son Lackie to protect her and her five youngest children: George; Henry Laurens, who was twelve years old in 1781; John Hampden, eleven; Esther, ten; and Catherine.

When Lachlan learned that his wife had left Camden, he expressed regret. Even if the family had fallen into British hands, he wrote to Sarah, "you could not be much more injured than you have been already." Traveling nearly three hundred miles from home with a large family and few conveniences was, he wrote, "sufficiently distressing without attempting to fly further." Nevertheless, he was happy that Sarah and all the children were in good health and were safe at Salisbury, North Carolina. He hoped they could stay at Salisbury "until we see what time brings forth." Lachlan sent instructions for his son Lackie to stay with Sarah and the younger children and "give every assistance in his power to the family, an indulgence which I think cannot be refused by any officer who commands the Southern Army." Lachlan asked Sarah and Lackie to "inform me of your situation by way of the Army."[29]

Despite Lachlan's wish that his wife and younger children would stay put, they continued to roam the South seeking refuge. They were, he said, "drove from place to place before the enemy many hundred miles, without any means to convey them, and obliged to exist on the bounty of such as might wish to assist."[30]

Lachlan's brother-in-law Robert Baillie wrote that he was "most anxious" to know the situation facing Sarah and the children. "I hope you will now be able to have them with you," Baillie told Lachlan, because "her present situation in North Carolina is very disagreeable, as it has been the seat of war."[31]

In 1781 Sarah and the children were stranded at Hillsboro, North Carolina, "in very great distress."

Lachlan's fellow prisoners of war included officers from Virginia who petitioned Virginia Governor Thomas Jefferson to assist the McIntosh family. The officers reminded Jefferson that McIntosh had commanded the Western Department, which included "the western part of our state," and that "the good effects" of his command "are still felt and acknowledged by our back inhabitants." As a result of the officers' petition, the Virginia Assembly appropriated funds to assist the McIntosh family. "The seasonable relief which my distressed family has lately received... will contribute to clothe and support us for some time," Sarah wrote Jefferson on April 23, 1781. She assured him that she would "consult all possible economy in its expenditure."[32]

A friend in Amherst County, Virginia, informed Lachlan in October of 1781 that "all your good family are in fine health, and are about to remove up here to a plantation which Col. Habersham has provided for them, as they are badly situated at present on land of a great villain Mat Marable in the upper end of Mecklenburg County about 90 miles from here. I mentioned that the principal wants of your little ones this winter would be blankets and clothes." The friend said that a "lieutenant in our county is particularly anxious to serve you and will furnish your family with bacon, corn, wheat." The lieutenant would not expect payment for the provisions until McIntosh was "peaceably established in Georgia."[33]

After being a prisoner of war for almost two years, McIntosh was exchanged in February of 1782.[34] He hurried to see his wife and children in Virginia, where they had ended up after enduring "a pursuit by the enemy of seven or eight hundred miles."[35]

The British garrison at Savannah evacuated on July 11, 1782, leaving Georgia in possession of the patriots. William McIntosh was elected to the Georgia Assembly and served on a committee negotiating a cessation of raids back and forth across the border with Florida, which remained a British colony.[36] This negotiation was important to the McIntosh brothers because their plantations were just north of the border. William had been involved in raids and counter-raids across the border since his childhood, when Florida was Spanish territory, and continuing during his service as a patriot officer during the American Revolution. With the Revolution coming to a close, he was ready for peace.

Lachlan McIntosh was fifty-five years old when he returned to Georgia in August of 1782 "to try if I can to pick up any of my wrecked property."[37] He found his plantation at Darien in ruins and his finances in shambles. His house at Savannah had not only been damaged during the siege but also had been sold during the British occupation, and he had to take legal action to get it back.

His wife and younger children, meanwhile, remained in exile. A deposition noted that Lachlan "returned to this State after an absence of near five years" – counting his service at Valley Forge and in the Western Department as well as his time as a prisoner of war – "his family then in

Virginia and his affairs much deranged by the War which required all his attention, in his advanced stage of life."[38]

While Lachlan focused on affairs in Georgia, his wife and children relocated from Virginia to Camden, South Carolina, where they were taken care of by family friends. As Lachlan anticipated welcoming his family home, tragedy struck – Lackie became ill and died in Camden on February 15, 1783, at the age of twenty-five.[39]

Lachlan McIntosh viewed his suspension from command as an attack on his personal honor. He worked tirelessly to restore his honor, beginning while he was a prisoner of war and continuing after he returned to Georgia. While confined at Haddrell's Point, he gathered support from fellow prisoners who had served with him in the Savannah campaign two years earlier. The officers declared themselves "highly satisfied" with General McIntosh as a gentleman and as a commanding officer. They reported hearing "the people in general make frequent and public avowals of their good opinion of the General." Political attacks on McIntosh, they said, "were dictated from principles that have produced the highest injustice to the General."[40]

The few officers remaining in the Georgia brigade of the Continental Army in May of 1780, including Lachlan's son Captain William McIntosh and nephew Lieutenant Colonel John McIntosh, signed a declaration at Augusta supporting their former commander. The Georgia officers accused politicians of making "unjust, ungenerous and malicious attacks upon the character of General McIntosh." In response to the attacks, the officers described McIntosh as not only a brave, humane, and circumspect military commander but also a tenacious American patriot. If they could choose any officer in the Continental army as their commander, they said, they would choose General McIntosh.[41]

Samuel Elbert, who had served as second in command while McIntosh commanded in Georgia, consistently showed respect for McIntosh. "I wish you to know," Elbert told McIntosh, "that I have constantly viewed you in the light of a zealous patriot and brave soldier, and that it has ever been with the greatest cheerfulness I have served under you."[42]

When McIntosh arrived in Philadelphia as a prisoner of war on parole in 1781, he was still seething with resentment over being suspended from command. He went before Congress and stated his case. Congress promptly rescinded the suspension.

After returning to Georgia, McIntosh directed his ire at George Walton, who had carried to Congress the documents that instigated the suspension. McIntosh and Walton had been friends and colleagues early in the war, when McIntosh commanded the Continental troops in Georgia and Walton represented Georgia in the Continental Congress. "I am much obliged to you," McIntosh had written Walton in 1776, "and very sensible of your friendship, which I can assure you is reciprocal, & may be put to the test on both sides."[43] During the period when a feud had raged between McIntosh and Button Gwinnett,

Walton had written to McIntosh "I freely confess to you my dear General that some pains have been taken to shake my friendship for your virtues and to lessen the good opinion of the Continent – but be assured that they never obtained credit with either."[44]

By 1779 Walton had expressed personal animosity toward McIntosh. "Mr. Walton said he had made General McIntosh," a witness recalled, "and he would be *Damned* if he would not break him."[45] A variation on that statement was provided by an official who "often heard George Walton declare he would have General McIntosh broke!"[46]

Colonel Robert Middleton, who had been a member of the executive council during Walton's term as governor, recalled that McIntosh had been "universally esteemed and respected except by George Walton." Middleton had "often heard" Walton "declare that he would have the General removed." During the sessions prior to McIntosh's suspension, Middleton said, "no act or resolution" had been passed "that tended or in any way construed to the prejudice of General McIntosh, nor any representation made or directed to be made to Congress respecting the General by the Legislature or Executive, nor any complaints made to either by the citizens or military during his stay in the state."[47]

When Walton was nominated as Chief Justice of Georgia in 1783, Lachlan's son William declared Walton to be "a coward and a villain" and threatened to "assist in pulling him off the bench, which ought to be filled with an unblemished character."[48]

Soon after issuing the declaration, William saw Walton walking with six friends through the streets of Savannah. William attacked Walton "with no other weapon but the horse whip, which I must confess was well laid on, without interruption from himself or any other person until he ran quite through the gate." William, an officer in the army, "was determined not to disgrace" his military sword "by using it on such an occasion." William claimed Walton "was corrected suitable to his demerit, and is evident & known proven to the whole town that he expected it, as I was under solemn promise to give it to him before he was put into any office the first opportunity I had, & conscious himself how much he deserved it."[49] Walton's offense, William made clear, was "his own infamous and personal behavior to my Father."[50] When William prepared to defend himself in a court martial, he insisted "my commission or my life are not equal to my honor."[51]

The Georgia Assembly gave McIntosh the vindication he sought. On February 1, 1783, the Assembly pronounced the letter to Congress that resulted in McIntosh's suspension from command to be "a forgery, in violation of law and truth and highly injurious to the interest of the State and dangerous to the rights of its citizens." The Assembly resolved "That General McIntosh be informed that this House do entertain an abhorrence of all such ungenerous attempts" to besmirch his character.[52]

In February of 1784 Congress praised McIntosh as "a worthy and brave officer who has served the United States with great reputation for near eight years" and promoted him to the rank of major general.[53]

Lachlan and Sarah McIntosh lived in Savannah after the war and established a plantation on Skidaway Island.[54] Lachlan still owned property in the Darien area and maintained a business partnership with Henry Laurens involving land along the Altamaha.

McIntosh resumed his role as a member of the coastal land-owning aristocracy. His social activities included serving as president of Savannah's Society of St. Andrew, which celebrates Scottish ancestry. Turning his attention from warhorses to race horses, he became an officer in the Liberty County Jockey Club. In political matters, he was appointed to several commissions and served a term in the Georgia Assembly.

Along with his political duties and social activities, McIntosh enjoyed associating with military veterans. Shortly after the war, officers who had served in the Continental Army formed the Society of the Cincinnati. When the Georgia chapter of the Cincinnati was founded, the officers who had served under McIntosh showed their respect for him by choosing him as their president. He made his priorities clear in 1784 when he was elected to Congress but did not go to Philadelphia to take his seat because at the time he was involved in an effort to obtain land in Georgia for his fellow war veterans.[55]

In the spring of 1791, Lachlan McIntosh enjoyed a reunion with George Washington, his former commander in the

Continental Army who had taken office as the first President of the United States. McIntosh and Washington held long-standing respect for one another. McIntosh had served with Washington during the terrible winter at Valley Forge. Then Washington had assigned McIntosh the difficult, if not impossible, task of pacifying the northwest frontier. When McIntosh had endured censure from his political enemies, Washington had not wavered in his regard for McIntosh.

During President Washington's tour of the southern states, McIntosh and four other men welcomed Washington at Purrysburg on the north bank of the Savannah River. A flotilla of boats and an eight-oared presidential barge transported the presidential party to Savannah. A joyful crowd welcomed the president while a band played "The Hero Comes." Artillery salutes roared from batteries on shore and on ships in the harbor. McIntosh and other members of the Order of the Cincinnati along with various civic leaders and military units escorted Washington to lodging on St. James Square.[56]

McIntosh participated in most of the events Washington attended during three days in Savannah. As a member of the Cincinnati, McIntosh was invited to dine with Washington and other dignitaries on the evening Washington arrived in Savannah. The men drank fifteen toasts, and the artillery company fired field pieces after each toast. Washington then retired for the evening, and the Georgians drank one more toast to the President of the United States.

The next day, a committee that included McIntosh presented an address. Washington provided proof, the committee observed, that "the virtues and talents of soldier and republican statesman will sometimes dwell together." The committee praised Washington for "having accomplished the great objects of a war, marked in its progress with events that astonished while they instructed the world." Because of Georgia's "exposed situation" on the southern frontier, the committee noted, the state "has been peculiarly affected by the calamities of war, but which, under the influences of a happy government, will rise fast to that rank of prosperity and importance to which her natural advantages so justly entitle her, and which will enable her to reflect back upon the Union all the benefits derived from it."[57]

In his reply, Washington observed that Georgia was "no less distinguished by its services than by its sufferings in the cause of freedom."[58]

Later in the day, Washington dined with the Georgia chapter of the Cincinnati, and proposed a toast to "The Members of the Society of the Cincinnati throughout the globe." That evening, as Washington noted in his diary, he attended a dance graced with a hundred "well dressed handsome ladies."[59]

McIntosh showed Washington the site where allied forces had assaulted British positions in 1779. A chronicle of Washington's Southern Tour reported: "As it fortunately chanced, General McIntosh had been second in command to General Lincoln at the time of the storming of the works; and gave the President a detached and lively account of the principal events of interest which happened during the siege and attack of the city."[60]

As nineteenth-century Georgia historian Charles C. Jones, Jr., has pointed out, "The earth mounds covering the slain, the lines of circumvallation, the sand parapets and gun chambers, had not then yielded to the influences of time and an encroaching population. The scars of the siege were still upon the bosom of the plain, and some of the houses within the limits of the city bore the marks of the lethal missiles which were then hurled. About him stood those who had passed through that baptism of fire. The President exhibited a deep interest in everything he then saw and heard."[61]

After touring the battleground, Washington addressed the people of Georgia. "While the virtuous conduct of your citizens, whose patriotism braved all the hardships of the late war, engaged my esteem, the distress peculiar to the state of Georgia, after the peace, excited my deepest regret," Washington said. "It was with singular satisfaction I perceived that the efficacy of the general government could interpose effectual relief, and restore tranquility to so deserving a member of the Union. Your sentiments on this event are worthy of citizens, who, placing a due value on the blessings of peace, desire to maintain it on the immutable principles of justice and good faith."

Washington concluded with a benediction upon McIntosh and his neighbors, "May you individually be happy."[62]

Lachlan and Sarah McIntosh lived into old age surrounded by members of the McIntosh family. They had a dozen grandchildren, including a grandson named Lachlan, another named John Lachlan, and two granddaughters named Sarah.[63]

Their first-born child Jack, who had returned from Jamaica after the war, helped Lachlan with farming and business matters, and provided aid to his parents during a severe winter following poor harvests.[64]

Lachlan's older brother William remained in the area of Darien and St. Simon's Island. William's daughter Margery married James Spalding and lived on St. Simon's Island. William's son Lieutenant Colonel John McIntosh returned to Darien after the war, then moved to Florida and was imprisoned by Spanish authorities; after his release, he returned to the area of St. Simon's and Darien. William's daughter Barbara married Captain William McIntosh – a British officer who served as an emissary to the Creek Indians during the American Revolution – and lived on a plantation near Darien.[65]

Lachlan's close friend William Bartram wrote a letter in 1796 looking back over their lives. Bartram wished "Health and Tranquility" to McIntosh, whom he called "Venerable Father Friend" because the "paternal care and friendship which you and your excellent lady Mrs. McIntosh were pleased to confer on me" years ago "during my residence in Georgia" had left "permanent impressions on my mind."

Bartram fondly recalled "those happy scenes, happy hours, which I enjoyed with your family." In his imagination, Bartram wrote, "I seem to be really in your happy family, enjoying with you that improving philosophic conversation you used to indulge me with."[66]

Lachlan McIntosh died at his house in Savannah on February 20, 1806, thirteen days before his seventy-sixth birthday. He was survived by his wife, their sons George, Henry, and Hampden, and their daughters Esther Ward and Catherine McCauley Harris.[67] Sarah, who became known in Savannah as a "truly respectable old Lady," died at home on March 4, 1814.[68]

9

Persevering Efforts in the Defense of America

Lachlan McIntosh suffered not only setbacks to his military strategies but also smears to his reputation throughout the American Revolution, all the while worried about the welfare of his wife, children, brothers and sister. Yet he persevered.

Savannah historian Alexander A. Lawrence referred to McIntosh as "the soldier who stood up to misfortune so stoutly."[1] Lawrence evaluated McIntosh as "a man of larger mould than has been supposed. The trials and tribulations he underwent in the American Revolution would have broken a less indomitable spirit."[2]

McIntosh's strength in the face of adversity impressed Aedanus Burke. In October of 1781 Burke wrote McIntosh a letter saying: "When I see a man surrounded with what the world calls more than difficulties: Exile from country, splendid fortune, from family, with wants of almost every kind into the bargain, when such a man bears all this not only with constancy, but laughs at it with gaiety, you must not blame me if I envy him, when I see myself and see most of the World besides me incapable of it."[3]

At the beginning of the war McIntosh was given command of Georgia's Continental troops, but he could never recruit enough soldiers to bring the battalion to full strength. He established a string of forts to protect

Georgia's southern border, but British, loyalist and Indian opponents overran the forts and raided into Georgia. In one of the border battles, a bullet struck McIntosh in the heel and the wound festered for weeks. British and American troops ruined plantations in South Georgia belonging to Lachlan, his brothers and his sister.

Lachlan's younger brother George was arrested for treason, thrown in jail briefly, and had his plantations confiscated by political enemies of the McIntosh family. In response, Lachlan called Button Gwinnett a scoundrel and lying rascal, was challenged by Gwinnett to a duel, and not only inflicted a wound that led to Gwinnett's death but also suffered a wound to his thigh. Gwinnett's supporters called for Lachlan to be removed from command, and he transferred to George Washington's army. While with Washington, he endured the terrible winter at Valley Forge.

Georgia historian William Bacon Stevens has blamed the feuding that caused McIntosh to leave Georgia in 1777 for Robert Howe's subsequent loss of Savannah in 1778 and John Ashe's debacle at Brier Creek in 1779: "How unfortunate it was for Georgia that she should have had in her armies as her defenders such men as Howe and Ashe, men totally incapacitated for the responsible duties, and whose errors and cowardice brought disgrace and ruin upon the State. Had not the wretched spirit of faction driven McIntosh from our borders, a different story might have been told of the British operations in Georgia."[4]

Washington assigned McIntosh command of the Western Department, where McIntosh once again planned a string of forts along a contested frontier. When Indians who were allied with the British besieged the outermost fort, McIntosh personally led a relief column at breakneck speed through rugged snow-covered terrain. Once again his ability as a military commander was subjected to criticism and once again he transferred to another department; this time back to the South.

While commanding the Western Department, according to *The Encyclopedia of the American Revolution,* McIntosh "showed a combination of incompetence and inability to handle subordinates."[5]

A Pennsylvania historian, however, offered a kinder view of McIntosh's tenure in the West: "Long range appraisal of all the evidence available has vindicated McIntosh's military acumen and the wisdom of his policy. He has been vindicated in other ways from a stigma that attached to him and seemed never to have been dispelled during his lifetime."[6]

A Wisconsin historian concluded that "the representation of McIntosh's inefficiency made to Washington by the officers' clique had done their work, and his recall was determined upon. News from Georgia of a British invasion and his family's peril, as well as discouragement with western conditions, made the recall seem to the General a release from an intolerable situation. Nevertheless, stung by the misrepresentations of his conduct during the campaign, after his return to the main army he requested an official investigation. In view of the difficulty of securing the attendance of witnesses from Pittsburgh and the need for his services in the South, McIntosh reluctantly abandoned the opportunity for exoneration, therein showing both good judgment and patriotism."[7]

McIntosh wanted to return to the South to protect his family. He had moved his wife and children from Darien in vulnerable South Georgia to Savannah, a place that seemed safe from British intrusions. But the British sent a force by sea that captured Savannah and trapped the McIntosh family behind British lines. Then the Americans and their French allies besieged Savannah. When McIntosh begged the British commander to release his family, the request was rejected. Sarah McIntosh and her children, like the other civilians in Savannah, huddled in basements while artillery from her husband's army bombarded the town. The siege concluded with an assault on Savannah that ended disastrously for the Americans and their allies. When the allies withdrew, the McIntosh family remained confined inside British lines.

After the family eventually was released, Lachlan took Sarah and the children to Camden, South Carolina, where he thought they would be safe. He then participated in the defense of Charleston. While there, he received word that his political enemies in Georgia had once again smeared his reputation and that Congress had suspended him from command of Continental troops. He was taken prisoner when Charleston fell to British besiegers. McIntosh had witnessed two of the most disastrous defeats of the Revolution, the assault on Savannah and the capture of Charleston.

When British forces moved toward Camden, the McIntosh family fled once again. The family wandered across North Carolina before finding refuge in Virginia. While McIntosh endured "severe imprisonment"[8] for more than a year, he asked his son Lackie to protect Sarah and the children. As warfare slowly subsided, Lachlan returned to Georgia while Sarah and the children found refuge once again in Camden, where Lackie became ill and died.

Yet McIntosh persevered.

As the war ground to an end in 1783, the Georgia Assembly recognized McIntosh as "an officer and citizen of this state who merits the attention of the Legislature for his early decided and persevering efforts in the defense of America."[9] A year later, nine officers who had served with McIntosh resolved "that the General from his unwearied attention and perseverance for the interest of the officers and soldiers under his command merit their warmest acknowledgements, therefore beg leave to return to him their thanks in behalf of themselves, their brother officers and soldiers."[10]

Lachlan McIntosh persevered.

Notes

Notes to Chapter 1:
EXPOSED BY LAND AND WATER TO ENEMIES

[1] Lachlan McIntosh to George Washington, Savannah, Georgia, March 8, 1776, *Papers of Lachlan McIntosh, 1774-1779*, ed. Lilla M. Hawes (Savannah: Georgia Historical Society, 1957), 1.

[2] McIntosh to Washington, March 8, 1776, 1.

[3] McIntosh to Washington, March 8, 1776, *2.*

[4] McIntosh to Washington, March 8, 1776, *2.*

[5] McIntosh to Washington, March 8, 1776, *2.*

[6] McIntosh to Washington, March 8, 1776, *2.*

[7] McIntosh to Washington, March 8, 1776, *2-3.*

[8] McIntosh to Washington, March 8, 1776, *3.*

[9] McIntosh to Washington, March 8, 1776, *3.*

[10] McIntosh to Washington, March 8, 1776, *3.*

[11] McIntosh to Washington, March 8, 1776, *3.*

[12] Walter J. Fraser, Jr., *Savannah in the Old South* (Athens: University of Georgia Press, 2003), 113-17; Harvey H. Jackson, *Lachlan McIntosh and the Politics of Revolutionary Georgia* (Athens: University of Georgia Press, 1979), 37-38.

[13] Martha Condray Searcy, *The Georgia-Florida Contest in the American Revolution, 1776-1778* (University, Ala.: University of Alabama Press, 1985), 34-36.

[14] Samuel Elbert to Charles Lee, Savannah, May 14, 1776, *Papers of Lachlan McIntosh*, 6.

[15] Edward J. Cashin, *William Bartram and the American Revolution* (Columbia: University of South Carolina Press, 2000), 231; Martha Condray Searcy, *The Georgia-Florida Contest in the American Revolution, 1776-1778* (University, Ala.: University of Alabama Press, 1985), 37.

[16] Searcy, *Georgia-Florida Contest,* 39.

[17] Searcy, 46.

[18] William Moultrie, *Memoirs of the American Revolution,* 1802 (New York: The New York Times & Arno Press, 1968), 1: 177.

[19] Moultrie, 1:179.

[20] Moultrie, 1: 179.

[21] Moultrie, 1: 180.

[22] Lachlan McIntosh to George Walton, Savannah, July 11, 1776, *Papers of Lachlan McIntosh*, 8.

[23] Lawrence, "Suspension," 108-09; Cashin, *Bartram,* 258.

[24] Cashin, *Bartram,* 235.

[25] Lachlan McIntosh Jr. to Lachlan McIntosh, Darien, July 22, 1776, *Papers of Lachlan McIntosh,* 52.

[26] Lachlan McIntosh Jr. to Lachlan McIntosh, July 22, 1776, 52-53.

[27] Lachlan McIntosh Jr. to Lachlan McIntosh, Darien, July 27, 1776, *Papers of Lachlan McIntosh,* 53-54.

[28] Lachlan McIntosh Jr. to Lachlan McIntosh, July 27, 1776, 53.

[29] Cashin, *Bartram,* 233.

[30] Cashin, *Bartram,* 233.

[31] Cashin, *Bartram,* 232.

[32] Lachlan McIntosh to Charles Lee, Savannah, July 29, 1776, *Papers of Lachlan McIntosh*, 10-11.

[33] Jackson, *Lachlan McIntosh,* 43.

[34] Frank Moore, *Diary of the American Revolution* (New York: New York Times and Arno Press, 1969), 1: 283-84.

[35] Lee to Armstrong, August 17, 1776, quoted in Jackson, *Lachlan McIntosh*, 44.

[36] Searcy, *Georgia-Florida Contest,* 56.

[37] Searcy, *Georgia-Florida Contest,* 56, 61-62; Kenneth Coleman, *The American Revolution in Georgia* (Athens: University of Georgia Press, 1958), 102.

[38] Searcy, *Georgia-Florida Contest,* 64-65.

[39] Lachlan McIntosh to Robert Howe, October 29, 1776, *Papers of Lachlan McIntosh*, 17-18.

[40] Lachlan McIntosh to William McIntosh, Savannah, October 22, 1776, *Papers of Lachlan McIntosh*, 15-16.

[41] Searcy, *Georgia-Florida* Contest, 68; Gordon Burns Smith, Morningstars of Liberty: The Revolutionary War in Georgia 1775-1783 (Milledgeville, Georgia: Boyd Publishing, 2006), 1:64-65.

[42] Searcy, *Georgia-Florida* Contest, 68.

[43] Lachlan McIntosh to Archibald Bulloch, November 1, 1776, *Papers of Lachlan McIntosh*, 57-58.

[44] Lachlan McIntosh to Robert Howe, Savannah, November 19, 1776, *Papers of Lachlan McIntosh*, 19.

[45] Lachlan McIntosh to Robert Howe, December 13, 1776, *Papers of Lachlan McIntosh*, 22-23.

[46] Searcy, *Georgia-Florida Contest,* 76-78.

[47] Searcy, 76-78.

[48] Searcy, 76-78.

[49] Robert W. Gibbes, *Documentary History of the American Revolution* (Spartanburg, S.C.: Reprint Company, 1972), 2: 51-52.

[50] Lachlan McIntosh to James Screven, February 19, 1777, *Papers of Lachlan McIntosh,* 41.

[51] McIntosh to Screven, February 19, 1777, 42.

[52] Lachlan McIntosh to John Habersham, Headquarters, February 20, 1777, *Papers of Lachlan McIntosh,* 42.

[53] Lachlan McIntosh to George Washington, Savannah, April 13, 1777, *Papers of Lachlan McIntosh*, 46.

[54] Lachlan McIntosh to George Washington, April 13, 1777, 46.

[55] Jackson, *Lachlan McIntosh*, n. 168; Searcy, *Georgia-Florida Contest,* 84-88; Lachlan McIntosh to George Washington, April 13, 1777, 46.

[56] Searcy, *Georgia-Florida Contest,* 84-88; Lawrence, "Suspension," 112.

[57] Jackson, *Lachlan McIntosh*, 55.

Notes to Chapter 2:
MR. MCINTOSH'S FAMILY

[1] William Stephens, "Journal of the Proceedings in Georgia Beginning October 20, 1737," in *Colonial Records of the State of Georgia*, ed. Allen D. Candler (New York: AMS Press, 1970). 4: 165.

[2] Albert S. Britt and Lilla M. Hawes, eds., "The Mackenzie Papers, Part II," *Georgia Historical Quarterly* 57.1 (1973): 111.

[3] Thomas Spalding, "Lachlan McIntosh, 1725-1806: Soldier" in *The National Portrait Gallery of Distinguished Americans,* 1867 (New York: Arno Press and The New York Times, 1970), 3:110.

[4] George White, *Historical Collections of Georgia,* 1855 (Baltimore: Genealogical Publishing Company, 1969), 334-35; Spalding, "Lachlan McIntosh," 103.

[5] Mills Lane, ed., *General Oglethorpe's Georgia: Colonial Letters. 1733-1743* (Savannah: The Beehive Press, 1975), 2: 437-39.

[6] Thomas Spalding, "Sketch of the life of General James Oglethorpe presented to the Georgia Historical Society" in *Collections of the Georgia Historical Society,* vol. 1 (Savannah: Georgia Historical Society, 1840), 271.

[7] *Colonial Records of Georgia* 35: 336-37.

[8] Quoted in Buddy Sullivan, *Early Days on the Georgia Tidewater: The story of McIntosh County & Sapelo* (Darien: McIntosh County Board of Commissioners, 1990), 34.

[9] Jackson, *Lachlan McIntosh*, 4-5.

[10] Spalding, "Lachlan McIntosh," 103.

[11] Larry Ivers, *British drums on the Southern Frontier: The Military Colonization of Georgia, 1733-1749* (Chapel Hill: The University of North Carolina Press, 1974), 206; Jackson, *Lachlan McIntosh*, 5.

[12] Jackson, *Lachlan McIntosh*, 5-6.

[13] George C. Rogers, "A Tribute to Henry Laurens," South Carolina Historical Magazine 92.4 (1991), 269-70.

[14] Spalding, "Lachlan McIntosh," 104.

[15] Lilla Mills Hawes, ed., *Lachlan McIntosh Papers in the University of Georgia Libraries (*Athens: University of Georgia Press, 1968), *82.*

[16] Walter Edgar, *South Carolina: A History* (Columbia: University of South Carolina Press, 1998), 161.

[17] Hawes, *Lachlan McIntosh Papers in the University of Georgia Libraries*, 3.

[18] *Register of Deaths in Savannah, Georgia*, Vol. 3, *August 1811-August 1818*, (Savannah: Georgia Historical Society, 1986), 79. According to the register, Sarah was seventy-four years old when she died on March 31, 1814, so she was sixteen or within a few months of turning sixteen when she married Lachlan on January 1, 1756.

[19] Jackson, *Lachlan McIntosh*, 8. Jackson writes, "By late 1756, McIntosh, his wife, and brother were back on the Altamaha... Shortly after the new year began, Sarah gave birth to her first child..."

[20] Hawes, *Lachlan McIntosh Papers in the University of Georgia Libraries,* 124-26; Smith, *Morningstars of Liberty*, 2: 167-68. Hawes gives the birth order, but not dates of birth. Smith, who includes an

impressive list of references, provides the year of birth for Lachlan Jr., William, Henry Laurens, and Esther. Both Hawes and Smith give the older daughter's name as Hester with Esther in parentheses; Smith notes that she was called "Hettie" or "Hetty." Hawes gives the name of Sarah McIntosh's mother as Esther in a note on page 124.

[21] Buddy Sullivan, *Supplemental Appendixes to Early Days on the Georgia Tidewater: The story of McIntosh County & Sapelo (Darien: McIntosh County Board of Commissioners,* 1991), 1.

[22] Hawes, *Lachlan McIntosh Papers in the University of Georgia Libraries,* 82-83.

[23] Edith Johnston, *The Houstouns of Georgia* (Athens: The University of Georgia Press, 1950), 346.

[24] Edward J. Cashin, *William Bartram and the American Revolution* (Columbia: University of South Carolina Press, 2000) 33.

[25] Cashin, *Bartram,* 34, 37; Sullivan, *Supplemental Appendixes,* 1.

[26] Bessie Lewis, *They Called Their Town Darien* (Darien, Ga.: The Darien News, 1975), 24. Alexander A. Lawrence, "General Lachlan McIntosh and His Suspension from Continental Command during the Revolution," *Georgia Historical Quarterly* 38.2 (1954), 104-5.

[27] Sullivan, Early Days, 46.

[28] Family Group Record for John Mor McIntosh, compiled by Mattie Gladstone, not published but copies may be available at the McIntosh County Historical Society office at Fort King George Historic Site at Darien, Georgia.

[29] Jackson, *Lachlan McIntosh,* 14-15.

[30] Jackson, *Lachlan McIntosh,* 15.

[31] Jackson, *Lachlan McIntosh,* 16.

[32] Johnston, *The Houstouns,* 345-47.

[33] Edith Johnston, *The Houstouns,* 346-47, 349; Jackson, *Lachlan McIntosh,* 17.

[34] Cashin, *Bartram,* 35; Sullivan, *Early Days,* 56.

[35] Cashin, *Bartram,* 35-37.

[36] Cashin, *Bartram,* 41-60.

[37] Cashin, *Bartram,* 66-67.

[38] Jackson, *Lachlan McIntosh,* 24.

[39] Sullivan, *Early Days*, 57.

[40] Jackson, *Lachlan McIntosh*, 25-29.

[41] Beryl I. Diamond, "Samuel Elbert (1740-1788)," *New Georgia Encyclopedia,* http://www.georgiaencyclopedia.org/search/advanced /samuel%20elbert (accessed August 22, 2017).

[42] Jackson, *Lachlan McIntosh*, 29-33.

[43] Jackson, *Lachlan McIntosh,* 4, 41.

[44] Mark M. Boatner III, *Encyclopedia of the American Revolution* (New York: David McKay Company, 1976), 692.

[45] Lawrence, "Suspension" 108-09; Cashin, *Bartram* 258.

[46] C.M. Destler, ed., "Unpublished letter of General Lachlan McIntosh," *Georgia Historical Quarterly* 23 *(*December 1929): 394-95.

[47] Johnston, *The Houstouns*, 348-51.

Notes to Chapter 3:
SLANDEROUS AND FALSE INSINUATIONS

[1] Lachlan McIntosh to Samuel Elbert, Headquarters, January 8, 1777, *Papers of Lachlan McIntosh,* 34.

[2] Lachlan McIntosh to Samuel Elbert, January 8, 1777.

[3] Searcy, *Georgia-Florida Contest,* 79, 88-90; Lawrence, "Suspension," 111; Jackson, *Lachlan McIntosh,* 54-55.

[4] Lachlan McIntosh to Samuel Elbert, January 8, 1777.

[5] Lachlan McIntosh to George Walton, Savannah, December 15, 1776, *Papers of Lachlan McIntosh*, 23.

[6] George Walton to Lachlan McIntosh, Philadelphia, April 18, 1777, quoted in Charles Francis Jenkins, *Button Gwinnett: Signer of the Declaration of Independence* (New York: Doubleday, Page & Company, 1926), 225.

[7] Johnston, *The Houstouns*, 351-52.

[8] *Case of George M'Intosh, Esquire,* (1777, Photostat Americana, Second Series, No. 160. Photostatted at the Massachusetts Historical Society, Boston, from the original in the Massachusetts Historical Society, August 15, 1942), 5.

[9] *Case of George M'Intosh, Esquire,* 12.

[10] *Case of George M'Intosh, Esquire,* 13.

[11] *Case of George M'Intosh, Esquire,* 13.

[12] *Case of George M'Intosh, Esquire,* 4-5.

[13] *Case of George M'Intosh, Esquire,* 5.

[14] *Case of George M'Intosh, Esquire,* 5.

[15] Johnston, *The Houstouns,* 352-54; Charles Francis Jenkins, *Button Gwinnett: Signer of the Declaration of Independence* (New York: Doubleday, Page & Company, 1926), 136.

[16] Johnston, *The Houstouns,* 352.

[17] Jackson, *Lachlan McIntosh,* 57.

[18] Jenkins, *Button Gwinnett,* 138-39.

[19] "The Case of George McIntosh," *Georgia Historical Quarterly* 3.3 (September 1919), 184.

[20] Johnston, *The Houstouns,* 354-55.

[21] Lachlan McIntosh to George Wells, Savannah, July 14, 1777, quoted in Jenkins, *Button* Gwinnett, 259.

[22] Lawrence, "Suspension," 113-14.

[23] Lachlan McIntosh to George Wells, Savannah, July 14, 1777, quoted in Jenkins, *Button* Gwinnett, 259.

[24] Hawes, *Papers of Lachlan McIntosh,* 62-63.

[25] Lachlan McIntosh to Henry Laurens, Savannah, May 30, 1777, quoted in Jenkins, *Button Gwinnett*, 254-55.

[26] *Case of George M'Intosh, Esquire,* 14-15.

[27] Johnston, *The Houstouns,* 107-342.

[28] *Case of George M'Intosh, Esquire,* 19.

[29] *Case of George M'Intosh, Esquire,* 20.

[30] *Case of George M'Intosh, Esquire,* 19.

[31] *Case of George M'Intosh, Esquire,* 21.

[32] *Case of George M'Intosh, Esquire,* 21.

[33] Johnston, *The Houstouns,* 351, 355-59.

[34] *Case of George M'Intosh, Esquire,* 21-22.

[35] *Case of George M'Intosh, Esquire,* 22.

[36] *Case of George M'Intosh, Esquire,* 22.

[37] *Case of George M'Intosh, Esquire,* 22.

[38] *Case of George M'Intosh, Esquire,* 13-14; Johnston, *The Houstouns,* 355, 357-58.

[39] Searcy, *The Georgia-Florida Contest,* 92-94.

[40] Jenkins, *Button Gwinnett*, 229.

[41] "George Wells' Affidavit respecting B.G. and L.M. June 1777," quoted in Edward G. Williams, ed. "A Revolutionary Journal and Orderly Book of General Lachlan McIntosh's Expedition, 1778," *The Western Pennsylvania Historical Magazine* 43 (1960): 3.

[42] "George Wells' Affidavit," 3.

[43] "George Wells' Affidavit," 3.

[44] "George Wells' Affidavit," 4.

[45] Marcus Holland, "Famous duel between Gwinnett, McIntosh to be played out again," *Savannah Morning News,* May 15, 1996, 7A.

[46] Lyman Hall to Roger Sherman, Savannah, June 1, 1777, quoted in Jenkins, *Button Gwinnett*, 229.

[47] Kenneth Coleman, *The American Revolution in Georgia* (Athens: University of Georgia Press, 1958), 87-89; E. Merton Coulter, *Georgia: A short history*, 3rd ed. (Chapel Hill: University of North Carolina Press, 1960), 134-35; Jackson, *Lachlan McIntosh,* 64-66.

[48] Lachlan McIntosh to Henry Laurens, Savannah, May 30, 1777, P.S., June 3, 1777, quoted in Jenkins, *Button Gwinnett,* 255.

[49] Lachlan McIntosh to Henry Laurens, Savannah, May 30, 1777, quoted in Jenkins, *Button Gwinnett,* 253.

[50] Lachlan McIntosh to Henry Laurens, Savannah, May 30, 1777.

[51] Ann Gwinnett to the Continental Congress, Savannah, August 1, 1777, quoted in Jenkins, *Button Gwinnett,* 238.

[52] Ann Gwinnett to John Hancock, Savannah, August 1, 1777, quoted in Jenkins, *Button Gwinnett,* 236.

[53] Searcy, *Georgia-Florida Contest,* 94.

[54] Searcy, *Georgia-Florida Contest,* 95.

[55] Searcy, *Georgia-Florida Contest,* 93-96.

[56] Searcy, 95-97.

[57] Searcy, 101.

[58] Hawes, *Lachlan McIntosh Papers at the University of Georgia Libraries,* 6.

[59] *Case of George M'Intosh, Esquire,* 23.

[60] *Case of George M'Intosh, Esquire,* 24.

[61] *Case of George M'Intosh, Esquire,* 7.

[62] *Case of George M'Intosh, Esquire,* 7-8.

[63] *Case of George M'Intosh, Esquire,* 7-8.

[64] *Case of George M'Intosh, Esquire,* 28.

[65] *Case of George M'Intosh, Esquire,* 27-28; Johnston, *The Houstouns,* 359-63.

[66] *Case of George M'Intosh, Esquire,*28.

[67] *Case of George M'Intosh, Esquire,* 28.

[68] *Case of George M'Intosh, Esquire,* 28-29.

[69] *Case of George M'Intosh, Esquire,* 28.

[70] *Case of George M'Intosh, Esquire,* 8; Johnston, *The Houstouns,* 359-63.

[71] Lachlan McIntosh to George Walton, Savannah, July 14, 1777, quoted in Jenkins, *Button Gwinnett,* 257, 260.

[72] *Addition to the Case of George McIntosh, Esquire* (1777), 6.

[73] George McIntosh, *Part of G McIntosh's Journal,* in *Lachlan McIntosh Papers in the University of Georgia Libraries,* ed. Lilla M. Hawes (Athens: University of Georgia Press, 1968), 94.

[74] George McIntosh, *Part of G McIntosh's Journal,* 95.

[75] *Addition to the Case of George McIntosh, Esquire* (1777), 6.

[76] Jenkins, *Button Gwinnett,* 162.

[77] George McIntosh, *Part of G McIntosh's Journal,* 95.

[78] George McIntosh, *Part of G McIntosh's Journal,* 95.

[79] George McIntosh, *Part of G McIntosh's Journal,* 95.

[80] *Addition to the Case of George McIntosh,* 9-10.

[81] Johnston, *The Houstouns,* 164.

[82] William Henry Drayton to John Adam Treutlen, August 1, 1777, *Documentary History of the American Revolution,* ed. R.W. Gibbes (Spartanburg, S.C.: The Reprint Company, 1972), 2: 86.

[83] Johnston, *The Houstouns,* 363-65.

[84] Hawes, *Lachlan McIntosh Papers in the University of Georgia Libraries,* 21.

[85] George C. Rogers, Jr., "A Tribute to Henry Laurens," *South Carolina Historical Magazine* 92.4 (1991): 274.

Notes to Chapter 4:
GREAT WORTH AND MERIT

[1] George Washington to the President of Congress, Valley Forge, May 12, 1778, *The Writings of George Washington from the Original Manuscript Sources 1745-1799,* ed. John C. Fitzpatrick (Washington: United States Government Printing Office, 1931-44), 11: 379.

[2] Jackson, *Lachlan McIntosh,* 71-73.

[3] Sullivan, *Early Days on the Georgia Tidewater,* 34; Hawes, *Lachlan McIntosh Papers in the University of Georgia Libraries,* 6, 21; Paul Lockhart, *The Drillmaster of Valley Forge: The Baron de Steuben and the Making of the American Army* (New York: Smithsonian Books, 2008), 76-77).

[4] Lockhart, *The Drillmaster of Valley Forge,* 84-85.

[5] George Washington to Lachlan McIntosh, Valley Forge, March 21, 1778, *Writings of George Washington,* 11: 120-21.

[6] Washington to McIntosh, March 21, 1778, 121.

[7] Jackson, *Lachlan McIntosh,* 73; Wayne Bodle, *The Valley Forge Winter: Civilians and soldiers in war* (University Park: The Pennsylvania State University Press, 2004), 214; Fitzpatrick, *Writings of George Washington,* 11: 120-21, 135-36.

[8] Jackson, *Lachlan McIntosh,* 73.

[9] Jackson, *Lachlan McIntosh,* 74-75.

[10] George Washington to the President of Congress, Valley Forge, May 12, 1778, *Writings of George Washington,* 11: 379.

[11] George Washington to William Russell, Valley Forge, May 19, 1778, *Writings of George Washington,* 11: 422.

[12] George Washington to Lachlan McIntosh, Valley Forge, *Writings of George Washington,* 11: 460-61.

[13] George Washington to Captain Lachlan McIntosh, Head Quarters, May 27, 1778, *Writings of George Washington,* 11: 461-62.

[14] Kellogg, *Frontier Advance,* 60-61; Edward G. Williams, ed., "A Revolutionary Journal and Orderly Book of General Lachlan McIntosh's Expedition, 1778," *The Western Pennsylvania Historical Magazine* 43 (1960): 165.

[15] Jackson, *Lachlan McIntosh,* 75-76.

[16] Jackson, 77.

[17] Jackson, 77-78.

[18] Jackson, 79; Kellogg, *Frontier Advance,* 148-49, 176.

[19] Hawes, *Papers of Lachlan McIntosh,* 75-77.

[20] Jackson 79-80; Kellogg 138-45; Ray Raphael, *A People's History of the American Revolution,* (New York: New Press, 2001), 214-17, 352.

[21] "Treaty with the Delawares, 1778," *The World Turned Upside Down: Indian Voices from Early America,* Colin G. Calloway, ed. (New York: Bedford Books, 1994), 192.

[22] Raphael, *People's History,* 216.

[23] Raphael, 216-17.

[24] "Treaty with the Delawares, 1778," 192-93.

[25] "Treaty with the Delawares, 1778," 191.

[26] Raphael, *People's History,* 352.

[27] Kellogg, *Frontier Advance,* 433.

[28] Williams, "Revolutionary Journal," 17; Kellogg, *Frontier Advance,*157.

[29] Jackson, *Lachlan McIntosh,* 80-81.

[30] Jackson 80-81; Williams, "Revolutionary Journal," 5-6.

[31] Kellogg, *Frontier Advance,* 437.

[32] Kellogg, 148.

[33] Williams, "Revolutionary Journal," 12; Jackson, *Lachlan McIntosh,* 84-85.

[34] Kellogg, *Frontier Advance*, 167-68; Williams, "Revolutionary Journal," 272-73.

[35] Williams, "Revolutionary Journal," 273.

[36] Williams, 14.

[37] Williams, 273.

[38] Williams, 274.

[39] Kellogg, *Frontier Advance,* 172-73.

[40] Williams, "Revolutionary Journal," 274.

[41] Williams, 274-75.

[42] Jackson, *Lachlan McIntosh*, 85, Williams, "Revolutionary Journal," 16.

[43] Williams, "Revolutionary Journal," 275-76.

[44] Williams, 16.

[45] Williams, 17.

[46] Jackson, *Lachlan McIntosh,* 85-86; Kellogg, *Frontier Advance,* 178-80.

[47] Williams, "Revolutionary Journal," 8.

[48] Williams, 276-77.

[49] Kellogg, *Frontier Advance,* 175.

[50] Daniel Agnew, *Fort McIntosh: Its Times and Men. "Fort Pitt" and Its Times. "Logstown,"on the Ohio*, 1893-1894 (Normal, Illinois: Normal Warfare Publications, 2007), 36; Kellogg, *Frontier Advance,* 294.

[51] Williams, "Revolutionary Journal," 287-88.

[52] Kellogg, *Frontier Advance,* 448.

[53] Williams, "Revolutionary Journal," 279.

[54] Williams, 281.

[55] Williams, 282.

[56] Kellogg, *Frontier Advance,* 160-61.

[57] Kellogg, *Frontier Advance,* 161.

[58] Kellogg, 185.

[59] Kellogg 451-52.

[60] Kellogg, 163.

[61] Kellogg, 161.

[62] Jackson, *Lachlan McIntosh,* 86; Kellogg, "Revolutionary Journal," 197.

[63] Lachlan McIntosh to George Bryan, Fort Pitt, December 29, 1778, *Frontier Advance on the Upper Ohio, 1778-1779,* ed. Louise Phelps Kellogg, 1916, (Charleston, S.C.: Bibliolife, 2011), 188-89.

Notes to Chapter 5:
EXTREME EMERGENCY AND DIFFICULTY

[1] "Recollections of Benjamin Buggs," in *Frontier Advance,* ed. Kellogg, 256-57.

[2] Louise Phelps Kell0gg, ed., *Frontier Advance on the Upper Ohio, 1778-1779,* (Lexington, KY: Bibliolife, 2011), 409.

[3] John Gibson to Lachlan McIntosh, Fort Laurens, December 21, 1778, *Frontier Advance on the Upper Ohio, 1778-1779,* ed. Louise Phelps Kell0gg (Lexington, KY: Bibliolife, 2011), 186.

[4] John Gibson to Lachlan McIntosh, Fort Laurens, January 1, 1779, *Frontier Advance on the Upper Ohio, 1778-1779,* ed. Louise Phelps Kell0gg (Lexington, KY: Bibliolife, 2011), 190.

[5] James Littell to William Littell, Fort McIntosh, January 29, 1779, "A Revolutionary Journal and Orderly Book of General Lachlan McIntosh's Expedition, 1778," ed. Edward G. Williams, *Western Pennsylvania Historical Magazine* 43 (1960): 162-63.

[6] Lachlan McIntosh to Archibald Lochry, Fort Pitt, January 29, 1779, *Frontier Advance,* ed. Kellogg, 210.

[7] Lachlan McIntosh to Richard Taylor, Fort Pitt, February 8, 1779, *Frontier Advance*, ed. Kellogg, 221.

[8] John Gibson to Lachlan McIntosh, Fort Laurens, February 13, 1779, *Frontier Advance*, ed. Kellogg, 226.

[9] Lachlan McIntosh to George Washington, Fort Pitt, March 12, 1779, *Frontier Advance*, ed. Kellogg, 240-42.

[10] Kellogg, *Frontier Advance,* 210.

[11] John Dodge to Congress, Pittsburg, January 25, 1779, *Frontier Advance,* ed. Kellogg, 208-09.

[12] Daniel Brodhead to George Washington, Fort McIntosh, January 16, 1779, *Frontier Advance,* ed. Kellogg, 200.

[13] George Washington to Daniel Brodhead, Head Quarters, February 15, 1779, *Frontier Advance,* ed. Kellogg, 230-31.

[14] George Washington to Gouverneur Morris, Middlebrook, March 20, 1779, *Frontier Advance,* ed. Kellogg, 262.

[15] Kellogg, *Frontier Advance,* 233.

[16] Lachlan McIntosh to Henry Laurens, Fort Pitt, March 13, 1779, *Frontier Advance,* ed. Kellogg, 251.

[17] McIntosh to Laurens, March 13, 1779, *Frontier Advance,* ed. Kellogg, 251.

[18] Lachlan McIntosh to Henry Laurens, Fort Pitt, March 13, 1779, *Frontier Advance,* ed. Kellogg, 250.

[19] "Recollections of Benjamin Buggs," in *Frontier Advance,* ed. Kellogg, 256-57.

[20] Lachlan McIntosh to George Washington, Fort McIntosh, March 19, 1779, *Frontier Advance,* ed. Kellogg, 256.

[21] McIntosh to Washington, March 19, 1779, *Frontier Advance,* ed. Kellogg, 256.

[22] McIntosh to Washington, March 19, 1779, *Frontier Advance,* ed. Kellogg, 256.

[23] John C. Dann, ed., *The Revolution Remembered* (Chicago: University of Chicago Press, 1980), 255.

[24] John Killbuck to Lachlan McIntosh, Cooshacking, March 13, 1779, *Frontier Advance,* ed. Kellogg, 248.

[25] "Recollections of Benjamin Buggs," in *Frontier Advance,* ed. Kellogg, 257.

[26] "Recollections of Henry Jolly," in *Frontier Advance,* ed. Kellogg, 257.

[27] Dann, *Revolution Remembered*, 255.

[28] Lachlan McIntosh to George Washington, Fort Pitt, April 3, 1779, *Frontier Advance,* ed. Kellogg, 270.

[29] Kellogg, *Frontier Advance*, 28, 233, 238, 271.

[30] Lachlan McIntosh to George Washington, Camp, May 14, 1779, *Frontier Advance,* ed. Kellogg, 327.

[31] Lachlan McIntosh to Alexander Hamilton, Camp, May 14, 1779, *Frontier Advance,* ed. Kellogg, 330.

[32] Alexander Hamilton to Lachlan McIntosh, Head Quarters, May 14, 1779, *Frontier Advance,* ed. Kellogg, 329.

[33] Lachlan McIntosh to Alexander Hamilton, Camp, May 14, 1779, *Frontier Advance,* ed. Kellogg, 329.

[34] George Washington to the President of the Continental Congress, May 11, 1779, quoted in Jackson, *Lachlan McIntosh*, 84.

[35] Lawrence, "Suspension," 121.

Notes to Chapter 6:
SHRIEKS FROM WOMEN AND CHILDREN

[1] Hawes, *Papers of Lachlan McIntosh*, 123-24.

[2] Benjamin Kennedy, ed., *Muskets, Cannon Balls & Bombs: Nine narratives of the Siege of Savannah in 1779* (Savannah: The Beehive Press, 1974), 128.

[3] Kennedy, 121.

[4] Kennedy, 121.

[5] Hugh McCall, *The history of Georgia: containing brief sketches of the most remarkable events, up to the present day,* 1811-16 (Atlanta: A.B. Caldwell, 1909), 2: 430.

[6] Kennedy, *Muskets*, 122-23.

[7] Alexander A. Lawrence, *Storm over Savannah: The story of Count d'Estaing and the Siege of the Town in 1779* (Athens: University of Georgia Press, 1951), 157.

[8] Hugh F. Rankin, *Francis Marion: The Swamp Fox* (New York: Thomas Y. Crowell Company, 1973), 35.

[9] Hawes, *Papers of Lachlan McIntosh*, 111.

[10] McCall, 2: 439.

[11] Lawrence, *Storm over Savannah*, 72.

[12] Jackson, *Lachlan McIntosh*, 98.

[13] Jackson, 98.

[14] Albert S. Britt Jr. and Lilla M. Hawes, eds., "The Mackenzie Papers, Part II," *Georgia Historical Quarterly* 57.1 (1973): 113-115.

[15] Kennedy, *Muskets,* 131.

[16] Kennedy, *Muskets,* 132.

[17] Robert Scott Davis, *Georgia Citizens and Soldiers of the American Revolution* (Greenville, S.C.: Southern Historical Press, 2000), 144.

[18] Davis, *Citizens and Soldiers*, 139.

[19] Kennedy, *Muskets,* 112.

[20] Kennedy, 110.

[21] Kennedy, 111.

[22] Kennedy, 112.

[23] Kennedy, 112-13.

[24] Kennedy, 113.

[25] Elizabeth Lichtenstein Johnston, *Recollections of a Georgia Loyalist,* 1836 (Spartanburg: The Reprint Company, 1974), 57-59.

[26] Kennedy, 109-114; Elizabeth Johnston, 59.

[27] William Harden, *A History of Savannah and South Georgia* (Atlanta: Cherokee Publishing Company, 1969), 1: 218.

[28] Kennedy, *Muskets,* 100.

[29] Harden, *History of Savannah,* 219.

[30] Harden, 219.

[31] Franklin B. Hough, ed., *The Siege of Savannah* (Spartanburg, S.C.: The Reprint Company, 1975), 84-85.

[32] Hough, *Savannah,* 71-73.

[33] Hough, *Savannah,* 84-85.

[34] Hough, *Savannah*, 173.

[35] Rupert Furneaux, *The Pictorial History of the American Revolution as told by Witnesses and Participants* (Chicago: JG. Ferguson, 1973), 299.

[36] Kennedy, *Muskets,* 73.

[37] Kennedy, 102.

[38] Kennedy, 101.

[39] Furneaux, *Pictorial History,* 300.

[40] Hough, *Savannah,* 167.

[41] Hough, *Savannah,* 167-68.

[42] Hough, *Savannah*, 168.

[43] Lawrence, *Storm*, 95.

[44] Kennedy, *Muskets*, 132.

[45] Jackson, *Lachlan McIntosh*, 103-04.

[46] *Case of George M'Intosh, Esquire, 8.*

[47] Johnston 363, 365; "Case of George McIntosh," *Georgia Historical Quarterly* 3.3 (September 1919): 137-88.

[48] Hawes, *Lachlan McIntosh Papers in the University of Georgia Libraries, 83-84.*

Notes to Chapter 7:
THE LAST EXTREMITY

[1] Lawrence, "Suspension," 122.

[2] Lachlan McIntosh, "Journal of the Siege of Charlestown, 1780," in *Lachlan McIntosh Papers in the University of Georgia Libraries University of Georgia Libraries: Miscellanea Publications, No. 7*, ed. Lilla Mills Hawes (Athens: University of Georgia Press, 1968), 96.

[3] McIntosh, "Journal of the Siege," 96.

[4] McIntosh, "Journal of the Siege," 97.

[5] McIntosh, "Journal of the Siege," 97.

[6] McIntosh, "Journal of the Siege," 97.

[7] McIntosh, "Journal of the Siege," 98.

[8] McIntosh, "Journal of the Siege," 98; Franklin B. Hough, ed., *The Siege of Charleston by the British Fleet and Army under the command of Admiral Arbuthnot and Sir Henry Clinton which terminated with the surrender of that place on the 12th of May, 1780*, 1867, (Spartanburg, S.C.: The Reprint Company, 1975), 79; Henry Lumpkin, *From Savannah to Yorktown: The American Revolution in the South*, (Columbia: University of South Carolina Press, 1981), *287.*

[9] McIntosh, "Journal of the Siege," 99.

[10] Williams, "Revolutionary Journal," 5-6.

[11] Kellogg, *Frontier Advance,* 190.

[12] Fitzpatrick, *Writings of George Washington,* 11: 388.

[13] Lawrence, "Suspension," 101-02.

[14] Lawrence, "Suspension," 101-02.

[15] McIntosh, "Journal of the Siege," 99.

[16] Jackson, *Lachlan McIntosh,* 105.

[17] Hawes, *Papers of Lachlan McIntosh*, 96.

[18] William Glascock to the President of Congress, Augusta, May 12, 1780, *Papers of Lachlan McIntosh*, ed. Lilla M. Hawes (Savannah: Georgia Historical Society, 1957), 91-92.

[19] Carl P. Borick, *A Gallant Defense: The Siege of Charleston, 1780* (Columbia: University of South Carolina Press, 2003), 104-06.

[20] Borick, *A Gallant Defense,* 126.

[21] Ed Southern, ed., *Voices of the American Revolution in the Carolinas* (Winston-Salem, N.C.: John F. Blair, 2009), 59.

[22] Lachlan McIntosh, "Journal of the Siege," 100.

[23] McIntosh, "Journal of the Siege," 100-01.

[24] McIntosh, "Journal of the Siege," 101.

[25] McIntosh, "Journal of the Siege," 102-03.

[26] McIntosh, "Journal of the Siege," 103.

[27] McIntosh, "Journal of the Siege," 104.

[28] McIntosh, "Journal of the Siege," 104.

[29] McIntosh, "Journal of the Siege," 104.

[30] McIntosh, "Journal of the Siege," 104-05.

[31] McIntosh, "Journal of the Siege," 105.

[32] McIntosh, "Journal of the Siege," 106.

[33] McIntosh, "Journal of the Siege," 106.

[34] McIntosh, "Journal of the Siege," 107-08.

[35] McIntosh, "Journal of the Siege," 106.

[36] McIntosh, "Journal of the Siege," 108.

[37] McIntosh, "Journal of the Siege," 109.

[38] McIntosh, "Journal of the Siege," 110.

[39] McIntosh, "Journal of the Siege," 110-11.

[40] McIntosh, "Journal of the Siege," 112.

[41] Jackson, *Lachlan McIntosh,* 110.

Notes to Chapter 8:
CALAMITIES OF WAR

[1] Lumpkin, *From Savannah to Yorktown,* 49.

[2] Carl P. Borick, *Relieve us of this burthen: American Prisoners of War in The Revolutionary South, 1780-1782* (Columbia: The University of South Carolina Press, 2012), 4-26; Borick, *A Gallant Defense,* 223.

[3] Moultrie, *Memoirs,* 2: 100-01.

[4] Moultrie, *Memoirs,* 2: 116.

[5] Moultrie, *Memoirs,* 2: 116.

[6] Moultrie, *Memoirs,* 2: 118.

[7] Moultrie, *Memoirs,* 2: 113.

[8] Lachlan McIntosh to Sarah McIntosh, Barracks at Haddrell's Point, South Carolina, August 7, 1780, *Lachlan McIntosh Papers in the University of Georgia Libraries,* ed. Lilla M. Hawes (Athens, University of Georgia Press, 1968), 41.

[9] Lachlan McIntosh to Sarah McIntosh, August 7, 1780, 41.

[10] Lachlan McIntosh to Sarah McIntosh, August 7, 1780, 41.

[11] Moultrie, *Memoirs,* 2: 119.

[12] Moultrie, *Memoirs,* 2: 119.

[13] Moultrie, Memoirs, 2: 132.

[14] Moultrie, *Memoirs,* 2: 130.

[15] Moultrie, *Memoirs,* 2: 134.

[16] Moultrie, *Memoirs,* 2: 135-36.

[17] Moultrie, *Memoirs*, 2: 148.

[18] Moultrie, *Memoirs,* 2: 164.

[19] Harvey, *Lachlan McIntosh, 122;* Hawes, *Lachlan McIntosh Papers in the University of Georgia Libraries,* 45.

[20] *Case of George M 'Intosh, Esquire,* 19.

[21] Robert Baillie to Lachlan McIntosh, St. Augustine, July 17, 1781, *Papers of Lachlan McIntosh,* ed. Lilla M. Hawes (Savannah: Georgia Historical Society, 1957), 98.

[22] Baillie to McIntosh, July 17, 1781, 98.

[23] Baillie to McIntosh, July 17, 1781, 100.

[24] Baillie to McIntosh, July 17, 1781, 99.

[25] Baillie to McIntosh, July 17, 1781, 98.

[26] Baillie to McIntosh, July 17, 1781, 98.

[27] Baillie to McIntosh, July 17, 1781, 99.

[28] Baillie to McIntosh, July 17, 1781, 98.

[29] Lachlan McIntosh to Sarah McIntosh, August 7, 1780, 41-42.

[30] Lachlan McIntosh to Congress, 1782, Hawes, *Papers of Lachlan McIntosh*, 107.

[31] Baillie to McIntosh, July 17, 1781, 99.

[32] Lawrence, "Suspension," 132-33.

[33] John Brickell to Lachlan McIntosh, 10 miles above Amherst Courthouse, Virginia, October 11, 1781, *Papers of Lachlan McIntosh,* 100-01.

[34] "Case of George McIntosh," *Georgia Historical Quarterly* 3.3 (September 1919): 139.

[35] "Case of George McIntosh," 137.

[36] Hawes, *Papers of Lachlan* McIntosh, 103-04.

[37] Lawrence, "Suspension," 132.

[38] "Case of George McIntosh," 139.

[39] Jackson, *Lachlan McIntosh,* 128.

[40] Continental Officers to McIntosh, January 7, 1781, *Lachlan McIntosh Papers in the University of Georgia Libraries,* 42, 45.

[41] "Declaration of Officers of the Georgia Line Respecting General McIntosh," *Lachlan McIntosh Papers in the University of Georgia Libraries,* 38-40.

[42] Samuel Elbert to Lachlan McIntosh, Philadelphia, January 18, 1782. *Papers of Lachlan McIntosh,* 84.

[43] Lachlan McIntosh to George Walton, Savannah, December 15, 1776, *Lachlan McIntosh Papers,* 22.

[44] George Walton to Lachlan McIntosh, Philadelphia, April 18, 1777, quoted in Jenkins, *Button Gwinnett,* 225.

[45] Hawes, *Lachlan McIntosh Papers,* 113.

[46] Hawes, *Lachlan McIntosh Papers,* 113.

[47] Hawes, *Lachlan McIntosh Papers,* 110.

[48] "Defense of Capt. William McIntosh before a General Court Martial, 1783," *Lachlan McIntosh Papers in the University of Georgia Libraries,* 58.

[49] "Defense of Capt. William McIntosh before a General Court Martial, 1783," 60.

[50] "Defense of Capt. William McIntosh before a General Court Martial, 1783," 63.

[51] "Defense of Capt. William McIntosh before a General Court Martial, 1783," 62.

[52] Allen. D. Candler, Revolutionary Records of the State of Georgia, (Atlanta: The Franklin-Turner Company, 1908), 3:248.

[53] Lawrence, "Suspension," 139.

[54] Jackson, *Lachlan McIntosh,* 130, 135.

[55] Jackson, 132-44.

[56] Archibald Henderson, *Washington's Southern Tour, 1791* (Boston: Houghton Mifflin Company, 1923), 208.

[57] Henderson, 212-13.

[58] Henderson, 214.

[59] Henderson, 218.

[60] Henderson, 220.

[61] Charles C. Jones Jr., ed. *The Siege of Savannah by the Fleet of Count D'Estaing in 1779*, 1874 (New York: The New York Times & Arno Press, 1968), 153-54.

[62] Henderson, 223.

[63] Albert S. Britt Jr. and Lilla M. Hawes, eds., "The Mackenzie Papers, Part II," *Georgia Historical Quarterly* LVII.1 (1973): 113-115; Orrin Sage Wightman, photographer, and story by Margaret Davis Cate, *Early Days of Coastal Georgia*St. Simon's Island, Georgia: Fort Frederica Association, 1955), 63.

[64] Jackson, *Lachlan McIntosh,* 147, 149.

[65] "Captain William McIntosh," *Ezell Family Tree*. 2 July 2013. <http://ezell.familytreeguide.com/getperson.php?personID=I10838&tree=T1>; Sullivan, *Early Days,* 34-37.

[66] Thomas Hallock and Nancy E. Hoffmann, eds., *William Bartram: The search for nature's design* (Athens: The University of Georgia Press, 2010), 181-83.

[67] *Abstracts of Wills, Chatham County, Georgia*, ed. Mabel Freeman La Far and Caroline Price Wilson (Washington, D.C.: National Genealogical Society, 1963), 97-98.

[68] *Register of Deaths in Savannah, Georgia*, vol. 3, 79.

Notes to Chapter 9:
PERSEVERING EFFORTS IN THE DEFENSE OF AMERICA

[1] Lawrence, "Suspension,"132.

[2] Lawrence, "Suspension," 104.

[3] Lawrence, "Suspension" 131-32.

[4] William Bacon Stevens, *A History of Georgia,* 1859 (Savannah: The Beehive Press, 1972), 2:197-98.

[5] Mark M. Boatner, III, *Encyclopedia of the American Revolution* (New York: David McKay Company, 1976), 693.

[6] Williams, "A Revolutionary Journal," 162.

[7] Kellogg, *Frontier Advance on the Upper Ohio,* 27.

[8] Lawrence, "Suspension," 131.

[9] Allen. D. Candler, Revolutionary Records of the State of Georgia, (Atlanta: The Franklin-Turner Company, 1908), 3:248.

[10] Hawes, *Papers of Lachlan McIntosh*, 129.

Bibliography

Addition to the Case of George McIntosh, Esquire, Earnestly recommended to the serious Attention of every Reader, particularly those of the State of Georgia. 1777. LOC copy. Scan from microfiche labeled 15384 provided by Interlibrary Loan Department of Brandeis University, Waltham, Mass.

Agnew, Daniel. *Fort McIntosh: Its Times and Men. "Fort Pitt" and Its Times. "Logstown,"on the Ohio.* 1893-1894. Normal, Illinois: Normal Warfare Publications, 2007.

American Revolution Roster: Fort Sullivan (later Fort Moultrie), 1776-1780. Charleston: Fort Sullivan Chapter of the Daughters of the American Revolution, 1976.

Boatner III, Mark M. *Encyclopedia of the American Revolution.* New York: David McKay Company, 1976.

Bodle, Wayne. *The Valley Forge Winter: Civilians and soldiers in war.* University Park: The Pennsylvania State University Press, 2004.

Borick, Carl P. *A Gallant Defense: The Siege of Charleston, 1780.* Columbia: University of South Carolina Press, 2003.

---. *Relieve us of this burthen: American Prisoners of War in The Revolutionary South, 1780-1782.* Columbia: The University of South Carolina Press, 2012.

Britt Jr., Albert S., and Lilla M. Hawes, eds. "The Mackenzie Papers, Part II." *Georgia Historical Quarterly* 57, no. 1 (1973): 113-115.

Campbell, Colin, ed. *Journal of an expedition against the rebels of Georgia in North America under the orders of Archibald Campbell Esquire Lieut. Colol. of His Majesty's 71ˢᵗ Regimt. 1778.* Augusta, Ga.: Richmond County Historical Society, 1981.

Candler, Allen. D. *Revolutionary Records of the State of Georgia.* 3 vols. Atlanta: The Franklin-Turner Company, 1908.

"(Captain) William McIntosh." *Ezell Family Tree.* 2 July 2013. <http://ezell.familytreeguide.com/getperson.php?personID=I10838&tree=T1>

Case of George M'Intosh, Esquire, A Member of the late Council and Convention of the State of Georgia; with The Proceedings thereon in the Hon. The Assembly and Council of that State. 1777. Photostat Americana, Second Series, No. 160. Copies located: Library of Congress; Massachusetts Historical Society. Photostated at the Massachusetts Historical Society, Boston, from the original in the Massachusetts Historical Society, August 15, 1942. Provided by the Interlibrary Loan Department of the College of William and Mary in Williamsburg, Virginia.

"Case of George McIntosh." *Georgia Historical Quarterly* 3, no. 3 (September 1919): 131-45.

Cashin, Edward J. *Lachlan McGillivray, Indian Trader: The shaping of the Southern Colonial Frontier*. Athens: University of Georgia Press, 1992.

--- *William Bartram and the American Revolution*. Columbia: University of South Carolina Press, 2000.

--- and Heard Robertson. *Augusta and the American Revolution: Events in the Georgia Back Country, 1773-1783*. Augusta, Ga.: Richmond County Historical Society, 1975.

Cate, Margaret Davis. *Our Todays and Yesterdays*. 1930. Spartanburg, S.C.: The Reprint Company, 1972.

Chernow, Ron. *Washington: A life*. New York: Penguin Press, 2010.

Coleman, Kenneth. *The American Revolution in Georgia*. Athens: University of Georgia Press, 1958.

"Colonel John McIntosh laid to rest for the third time in McIntosh Co." *The Darien News* 28 Oct. 2010: 1+

Colonial Records of the State of Georgia (CRG), 28 vols. 1904-10. New York: AMS Press, 1970.

Coulter, E. Merton. *Georgia: A short history*. Third Edition. Chapel Hill: University of North Carolina Press, 1960.

Dann, John C. *The Revolution Remembered: Eyewitness accounts of the War for Independence*. Chicago: University of Chicago Press, 1980.

Davis, Burke. *George Washington and the American Revolution*. New York: Random House, 1975.

Davis Jr., Robert Scott. *Encounters on a March Through Georgia in 1779: The Maps and Memorandums of John Wilson, Engineer, 71ˢᵗ Highland Regiment*. Sylvania, Ga.: Partridge Pond Press, 1986.

---. *Georgia Citizens and Soldiers of the American Revolution*. 1979. Greenville, S.C.: Southern Historical Press, 2000.

---. *Georgians in the Revolution: At Kettle Creek (Wilkes County) and Burke County*. Easley, S.C.: Southern Historical Press, 1996.

Dobson, David. *Directory of Scots in the Carolinas, 1680-1830*. Baltimore: Genealogical Publishing, 1986.

---. *Scottish Emigration to Colonial America, 1607-1785*. Athens: University of Georgia Press, 1994.

Diamond, Beryl I. "Samuel Elbert (1740-1788)." *New Georgia Encyclopedia*.

http://www.georgiaencyclopedia.org/search/advanced/s amuel%20elbert (accessed August22, 2017).

Dupuy, R. Ernest and Trevor N. Dupuy. *The Compact History of the Revolutionary War*. New York: Hawthorn Books, 1963.

Edgar, Walter. *South Carolina: A History*. Columbia: University of South Carolina Press, 1998.

Fitzpatrick, John C. *The Writings of George Washington from the Original Manuscript Sources 1745-1799*. 39 vols. Washington: United States Government Printing Office, 1931-44.

Frank, Andrew K. "The Rise and Fall of William McIntosh: Authority and Identity on the Early

American Frontier." *Georgia Historical Quarterly* 86.1 (Spring 2002): 18-48.

Fraser Jr., Walter J. *Savannah in the Old South*. Athens: University of Georgia Press, 2003.

Furneaux, Rupert. *The Pictorial History of the American Revolution as told by Witnesses and Participants*. Chicago: JG. Ferguson, 1973.

"Gen. Lachlan McIntosh (1727-1806)." *Georgia Historical Society*. 1 August 2017. <http://georgiahistory.com/gh mi_marker_updated/gen-lachlan-mcintosh-1727-1806/>

Gibbes, Robert W. *Documentary History of the American Revolution*. 1853-57. 3 vols. Spartanburg, S.C.: Reprint Company, 1972.

Gladstone, Mattie. Notes, manuscripts and photocopies related to McIntosh genealogy. The Ridge, Darien, Georgia: unpublished, personal communication, 1980 - 2002.

---. Family Group Record for John Mor McIntosh. Copies may be available at the McIntosh County Historical Society office at Fort King George Historic Site at Darien, Georgia.

---. Genealogical chart showing descendants of William Mackintosh, 3rd Proprietor of Borlum. Copies may be available at the McIntosh County Historical Society office at Fort King George Historic Site at Darien, Georgia.

George Wells' Affidavit respecting B.G. and L.M. June 1777, quoted in Edward G. Williams, ed. "A Revolutionary Journal and Orderly Book of General

Lachlan McIntosh's Expedition, 1778," *The Western Pennsylvania Historical Magazine* 43 (1960): 3-4.

Hallock, Thomas and Nancy E. Hoffmann, eds. *William Bartram: The search for nature's design.* Athens: The University of Georgia Press, 2010.

Hamer, Philip M., ed. *The Papers of Henry Laurens.* 9 vols. Columbia: University of South Carolina Press, 1968-81.

Harden, William. *A History of Savannah and South Georgia.* Vol. 1. Atlanta: Cherokee Publishing Company, 1969.

Hawes, Lilla M., ed. *Lachlan McIntosh Papers in the University of Georgia Libraries.* Series: *University of Georgia Libraries, Miscellanea Publications, No. 7.* Athens: University of Georgia Press, 1968.

---, ed. "The Papers of James Jackson 1781-1798." *Collections of the Georgia Historical Society Vol. XI.* Savannah: Georgia Historical Society, 1935.

---, ed. *The Papers of Lachlan McIntosh, 1774-1779.* Series: *Collections of the Georgia Historical Society Vol. XII.* Savannah: Georgia Historical Society, 1957.

Henderson, Archibald. *Washington's Southern Tour, 1791.* Boston: Houghton Mifflin Company, 1923.

Holland, Marcus. "Famous duel between Gwinnett, McIntosh to be played out again." *Savannah Morning News,* May 15, 1996, sec. A.

Hough, Franklin B., ed. *The Siege of Charleston by the British Fleet and Army under the command of Admiral Arbuthnot and Sir Henry Clinton which terminated with the surrender of that place on the 12ᵗʰ of May, 1780.* 1867. Spartanburg, S.C.: The Reprint Company, 1975.

---, ed. *The Siege of Savannah by the Combined American and French Forces under the command of Gen. Lincoln and the Count d'Estaing in the Autumn of 1779.* 1866. Spartanburg, S.C.: The Reprint Company, 1975.

Ivers, Larry E. *British Drums on the Southern Frontier: The military colonization of Georgia, 1733-1749.* Chapel Hill: The University of North Carolina Press, 1974.

Jackson III, Harvey Hardaway. *General Lachlan McIntosh, 1727-1806: A Biography.* Diss. University of Georgia, 1973. Athens: University of Georgia, 1973.

---. *Lachlan McIntosh and the politics of revolutionary Georgia.* 1979. Athens: University of Georgia Press, 2003.

Jenkins, Charles Francis. *Button Gwinnett: Signer of the Declaration of Independence.* New York: Doubleday, Page & Company, 1926.

Johnston, Elizabeth Lichtenstein. *Recollections of a Georgia Loyalist.* 1836. Spartanburg: The Reprint Company, 1974.

Johnston, Edith Duncan. *The Houstouns of Georgia.* Athens: The University of Georgia Press, 1950.

Jones Jr., Charles C., ed. *The Siege of Savannah by the Fleet of Count D'Estaing in 1779.* 1874. New York: The New York Times & Arno Press, 1968.

Kellogg, Louise Phelps, ed. *Frontier Advance on the Upper Ohio, 1778-1779*. 1916. Charleston, S.C.: Bibliolife, 2011.

Kennedy, Benjamin, ed. *Muskets, Cannon Balls & Bombs: Nine narratives of the Siege of Savannah in 1779*. Savannah: The Beehive Press, 1974.

Lane, Mills, ed. *General Oglethorpe's Georgia: Colonial Letters. 1733-1743*. 2 vols. Savannah: The Beehive Press, 1975.

La Far, Mabel Freeman and Caroline Price Wilson, eds. *Abstract of Wills, Chatham County, Georgia, 1773-1817*. 1933. Washington, D.C.: National Genealogical Society, 1963.

Lawrence, Alexander A. "General Lachlan McIntosh and His Suspension from Continental Command During the Revolution." *Georgia Historical Quarterly* 38, no. 2 (1954): 101-141.

---. "General Robert Howe and the British Capture of Savannah in 1778." *Georgia Historical Quarterly* 36, no. 4 (1952): 303-327.

---. *Storm over Savannah: The story of Count d'Estaing and the Siege of the Town in 1779*. Athens: University of Georgia Press, 1951.

Lewis, Bessie. *They Called Their Town Darien*. Darien, Ga.: The Darien News, 1975.

Lockhart, Paul. *The Drillmaster of Valley Forge: The Baron de Steuben and the Making of the American Army*. New York: Smithsonian Books, 2008.

Lumpkin, Henry. *From Savannah to Yorktown: The American Revolution in the South.* Columbia: University of South Carolina Press, 1981.

Mackintosh of Mackintosh, Margaret, revised by Lachlan Mackintosh of Mackintosh, 30th Chief of Mackintosh. *The History of Clan Mackintosh and Clan Chattan.* Edinburgh: The Pentland Press Limited, 1997.

Massey, Gregory D. *John Laurens and the American Revolution.* Columbia: University of South Carolina Press, 2000.

McCall, Hugh. *The history of Georgia: containing brief sketches of the most remarkable events, up to the present day.* 2 vols. 1811-16. Atlanta: A.B. Caldwell, 1909.

McIntosh, George. *Part of G. McIntosh's Journal.* In *Lachlan McIntosh Papers in the University of Georgia Libraries University of Georgia Libraries,* edited by Lilla Mills Hawes, 94-95. Athens: University of Georgia Press, 1968.

McIntosh, Lachlan. *Journal of the Siege of Charlestown, 1780.* In *Lachlan McIntosh Papers in the University of Georgia Libraries University of Georgia Libraries,* edited by Lilla Mills Hawes, 96-122. Athens: University of Georgia Press, 1968

Mitchell, Frances Letcher. *Georgia Land and People.* 1900. Spartanburg, S.C.: The Reprint Company, 1974.

Moore, Frank. *Diary of the American Revolution.* 2 vols. New York: New York Times and Arno Press, 1969.

Moultrie, William. *Memoirs of the American Revolution*. 2 vols. 1802. New York: The New York Times & Arno Press, 1968.

Parker, Anthony W. *Scottish Highlanders in Colonial Georgia: The recruitment, emigration, and settlement at Darien, 1735-1748*. 1997. Athens: University of Georgia Press, 2002.

Piechocinski, Elizabeth Carpenter. *The Old Burying Ground: Colonial Park Cemetery, Savannah, Georgia 1750-1853*. Savannah: The Oglethorpe Press, 1999.

Raphael, Ray. *A People's History of the American Revolution: How common people shaped the fight for independence*. New York: New Press, 2001.

Register of Deaths in Savannah, Georgia. Vol. 3, *August 1811-August 1818*. Savannah: Georgia Historical Society, 1986.

Rogers Jr., George C. "A Tribute to Henry Laurens." *South Carolina Historical Magazine* 92.4 (1991): 269-276.

Scheer, George F. and Hugh F. Rankin. *Rebels and Redcoats*. New York: The World Publishing Company, 1957.

Searcy, Martha Condray. *The Georgia-Florida Contest in the American Revolution, 1776-1778*. University, Ala.: University of Alabama Press, 1985.

Smith, Gordon Burns. *Morningstars of Liberty: The Revolutionary War in Georgia 1775-1783*. 2 vols. Milledgeville, Georgia: Boyd Publishing, 2006. 1:64-65.

Southern, Ed, ed. *Voices of the American Revolution in the Carolinas*. Winston-Salem, N.C.: John F. Blair, 2009.

Spalding, Thomas. "Lachlan McIntosh, 1725-1806: Soldier." *The National Portrait Gallery of Distinguished Americans*. Vol. 3. 1867. New York: Arno Press and The New York Times, 1970: 99-110.

---. "Sketch of the life of General James Oglethorpe presented to the Georgia Historical Society." *Collections of the Georgia Historical Society*. Vol. 1, 240-95. Savannah: Georgia Historical Society, 1840.

Stephens, William. "Journal of the Proceedings in Georgia Beginning October 20, 1737." In *Colonial Records of the State of Georgia*, ed. Allen D. Candler, Vol. 4, 5-662. New York: AMS Press, 1970.

Stevens, William Bacon. *A history of Georgia, from its first discovery by Europeans to the adoption of the present constitution in MDCCXCVIII*. 1847-1859. 2 vols. Savannah: The Beehive Press, 1972.

Stokes, Thomas L. *The Savannah*. 1951. Athens: University of Georgia Press, 1982.

Sullivan, Buddy. *Early Days on the Georgia Tidewater: The story of McIntosh County & Sapelo*. Darien: McIntosh County Board of Commissioners, 1990.

--- . Supplemental Appendixes. *Early Days on the Georgia Tidewater: The story of McIntosh County & Sapelo*. 1991.

Uhlendorf, Bernard A., trans. and ed. *The Siege of Charleston with an account of the province of South Carolina: Diaries and letters of Hessian officers from the von Jungkenn Papers in the William L. Clements Library*. Ann Arbor: University of Michigan Press, 1938.

Ward, Christopher. *The War of the Revolution*. 2 vols. Ed. John Richard Alden. New York: Macmillan, 1952.

White, George. *Historical Collections of Georgia*. 1855. Baltimore: Genealogical Publishing Company, 1969.

Wightman, Orrin Sage, photographer, and story by Margaret Davis Cate. *Early Days of Coastal Georgia*. St. Simons Island, Georgia: Fort Frederica Association, 1955.

Williams, Edward G., ed. "A Revolutionary Journal and Orderly Book of General Lachlan McIntosh's Expedition, 1778." *The Western Pennsylvania Historical Magazine* 43 (1960): 1-17, 157-77, 267-88.

Index